William Cranston Lawton

The New England Poets

A Study of Emerson, Hawthorne, Longfellow, Whittier, Lowell, Holmes

William Cranston Lawton

The New England Poets
A Study of Emerson, Hawthorne, Longfellow, Whittier, Lowell, Holmes

ISBN/EAN: 9783337279196

Printed in Europe, USA, Canada, Australia, Japan

Cover: Foto ©Thomas Meinert / pixelio.de

More available books at **www.hansebooks.com**

THE

NEW ENGLAND POETS

A Study of

EMERSON, HAWTHORNE, LONGFELLOW
WHITTIER, LOWELL, HOLMES

BY

WILLIAM CRANSTON LAWTON

AUTHOR OF "ART AND HUMANITY IN HOMER,"
"SUCCESSORS OF HOMER," ETC.

New York
THE MACMILLAN COMPANY
LONDON: MACMILLAN & CO., Ltd.
1898

All rights reserved

COPYRIGHT, 1898,
BY THE MACMILLAN COMPANY.

Norwood Press
J. S. Cushing & Co. — Berwick & Smith
Norwood Mass. U.S.A.

M. F. L.   E. B. L.
W. A. L.

καί ποτέ τις εἴποι 'πατρός γ' ὅδε πολλὸν ἀμείνων.'

PREFACE

AFTER twenty years devoted to the study and teaching of remoter and richer literatures, the demand for "University Extension" lectures first suggested a return to these earliest guides of our New England boyhood. Like that boyhood itself, these benignant figures have already something of the perspective which Time alone can bestow. Two of the six I never even saw. The men who, like Colonel Higginson and Professor Norton, have been our indulgent Mentors, were in their turn the younger associates of the group here discussed.

Nevertheless our Yankee loyalty throbs too warmly from heart to heart to permit mere cold analytical criticism. But must impartial or fruitful criticism be cold, remote, even semi-hostile? Can we not know aright, and fairly judge, those whom we love best, and to whom we owe most?

Katahdin is not Olympus. The Charles and the Merrimac know not the impetuous spring current of the Arno. Lowell's noblest ode has no Pindaric splendor. Longfellow's epics of dying civilizations cannot set Gabriel and Hiawatha beside Odysseus or Æneas. This, at least, we realize as clearly as Brunetière or Saintsbury could expound it.

But if literary criticism has a right to share in warm and kindly life at all, it may well obey the spirit of the Delphic command, and begin nearest home. These are our poets, the interpreters of our own life. We have loved them as long as we have shivered in the northeast wind, or welcomed the pale blossoms of March. The attempt to indicate the modest amount which they have contributed to the world's abiding wealth, may be defended as natural, loyal, and filial.

W. C. L.

ADELPHI COLLEGE, BROOKLYN,
    EASTER, 1898.

EMERSON	HAWTHORNE	LONGFELLOW
1803, *May 25.* Born in Boston.	1804, *July 4.* Born in Salem.	
		1807, *Feb. 27.* Born in Portland.
1817–21. Student at Harvard.		
		1820. "Battle of Lovell's Pond." (First poem printed.)
1821–26. *Taught school and studied theology.* 1823. "Good-by, proud world."	1821–25. *Student at Bowdoin.*	1821–25. *Student at Bowdoin College.* "Burial of Minnisink," etc.
1829–32. *Preacher in Second Church, Boston.* 1829. *First marriage.*	1826. Fanshawe	1826–29. *Studying in France, Spain, Italy, and Germany.* 1829. *Professor and Librarian, Bowdoin.*
1832. *Death of Mrs. Emerson.* 1833–34. *Travelled in Europe. Met Carlyle.* 1835. *Emerson's second marriage. Settled in Concord.* Lectured in Boston, on *English literature.* 1836. *Hymn at Concord Bridge.* NATURE. 1837. *Oration on the American Scholar.* 1838. *Divinity School Address.* 1840. "The Problem," in first number of *Dial.*	1831–35. Tales, published in "Token and Atlantic Souvenir." 1837. TWICE-TOLD TALES (Vol. I). 1839–41. *In Boston custom house.*	1831. *First marriage.* Origin and Progress of French Language. N.A.R. 1832. Defence of Poetry. N.A.R. History of Italian Language. N.A.R. 1833. Spanish Language and Literature. N.A.R. 1835. OUTRE-MER. 1835–36. *Travelling in England, Germany, and Scandinavia. Death of Mrs. L.* 1836, *Dec. Professor at Harvard.* 1838. Anglo-Saxon Literature. N.A.R. Psalm of Life. 1839. HYPERION. VOICES OF THE NIGHT. 1840. Skeleton in Armor.

WHITTIER	HOLMES	LOWELL	AMERICANA
			1805-11. Wm. Emerson edited *Monthly Anthology*.
1807, Dec. 17. Born in Haverhill.	1809, Aug. 29. Born in Cambridge.		1807. Joel Barlow's Columbiad.
			1812. Bryant's Thanatopsis written. (Published, 1817.)
			1815. Foundation of the *North American Review*.
		1819, Feb. 22. Born in Cambridge.	1819. Irving's SKETCH BOOK.
1822. Received Burns' poems as a present.			1821. Cooper's SPY. Bryant's first volume of POEMS.
1826. First published verses in Garrison's paper.	1824-25. Student at Andover. 1825-29. Student at Harvard.		1823. Birth of Col. Higginson and Francis Parkman.
1827-28. Taught school. 1828. Student in Haverhill Acad.	1830. Old Ironsides. Studied law a year.		1828. Webster's DICTIONARY.
1831. Legends of New England.	1831-33. Studied medicine at home.		
			1832. Death of Freneau. (Born 1752.)
1833. In Philadelphia at the formation of the Antislavery Society.	1833-36. Travelled, and studied medicine, chiefly in Paris.	1834-38. Student at Harvard.	1833. *The Knickerbocker*. (Until 1858.)
1835-36. Member of Mass. Legislature.			
	1836. POEMS (first collection).		1836. First meeting of the Transcendental Club.
	1839-40. *Prof. of Anatomy and Physiology*, Dartmouth College. Returned to Boston.	1838-40. Studied law at Harvard.	1837. Birth of Howells.
1840. Made his home in Amesbury.	1840. Married.	1840. A YEAR'S LIFE.	1840. Brook Farm Community organized.

EMERSON	HAWTHORNE	LONGFELLOW
1841. ESSAYS (Vol. 1). 1842-44. *Edited Dial.* 1842. *Death of his son Waldo, aged five.* (Threnody.) 1844. *Address on Emancipation.* ESSAYS (Vol. 2). 1846. POEMS. 1847-49. *Lectured in England on* REPRESENTATIVE MEN. (Published, 1850.)	1841. Grandfather's Chair. 1841-42. *At Brook Farm.* 1842. *Married.* 1842-46. *At Concord, in Old Manse.* 1845. TWICE-TOLD TALES (Vol. II). 1846. MOSSES. 1846-50. *In Salem custom house.* 1850. SCARLET LETTER.	1841. Excelsior. BALLADS AND POEMS. 1842. *An invalid in Germany, meets Freiligrath.* POEMS ON SLAVERY. 1843. SPANISH STUDENT. *Second marriage.* 1847. EVANGELINE. (Begun 1845.) 1849. KAVANAGH.
1856. ENGLISH TRAITS. 1857. "Brahma," in first number of *Atlantic Monthly*. 1859. Speech at the Burns' festival. 1860. CONDUCT OF LIFE.	1851. HOUSE OF SEVEN GABLES. Wonderbook. 1852. SNOW IMAGE. BLITHEDALE ROMANCE. Life of Pierce. 1852-53. *In Concord, at the Wayside.* 1853-57. *At Liverpool.* 1857-59. *Travelling, chiefly in Italy.* 1859-60. *In England.* 1860. MARBLE FAUN.	1851. GOLDEN LEGEND. (Begun 1850.) 1855. HIAWATHA. (Begun 1854.) 1858. MILES STANDISH. (Begun 1857.)
1866. Terminus. 1867. May-day.	†1864, *May. At Plymouth, N.H.*	1861. *Death of Mrs. L.* 1863. TALES OF A WAYSIDE INN. Part I. (Begun 1860.) 1868. NEW ENGLAND TRAGEDIES. 1868-69. *Last visit in Europe.* 1867-70. DANTE.
1872. *His house burned, and restored by friends.*		1872. CHRISTUS. 1874. Morituri Salutamus. AFTERMATH. 1878. KERAMOS. 1879. Cross of Snow. 1880. ULTIMA THULE.
†1882, *April. At Concord.*		†1882, *Mar. In Craigie House.*

WHITTIER	HOLMES	LOWELL	AMERICANA
		1844. "Conversations on Old Poets." Married. 1846-50. Writer for Antislavery Standard. 1847-48. BIGLOW PAPERS (First Series). 1848. FABLE FOR CRITICS. VISION OF SIR LAUNFAL.	1840-44. The Dial. 1840-47. Brook Farm Experiment. 1845. Poe's Raven. 1849. Death of Poe. (Born 1809.) 1850. Death of Margaret Fuller. (Born 1810.)
1847-57. Corresponding editor "National Era." 1849. "Margaret Smith's Journal." 1850. Songs of Labor.	1847. Elected Professor in Harvard Medical School.		
1857. COLLECTED POEMS. Made member of the Atlantic Circle.	1851. First class poem. 1852. Began Lyceum lectures, on British poets. 1857. AUTOCRAT, in first volume of the Atlantic (published 1859). 1860. PROFESSOR.	1851-52. In Europe. 1853. Mrs. L. died at Elmwood. (Longfellow's "Two Angels.") 1855. Professor at Harvard. 1856-57. Studying in Germany. 1857. Second marriage. Editor of Atlantic Monthly.	1851. Death of Cooper. (Born 1789.) 1851-52. UNCLE TOM'S CABIN. 1857. Foundation of the ATLANTIC MONTHLY. 1859. Irving died. (Born 1783.)
1865. SNOW-BOUND. 1867. TENT ON THE BEACH.	1861. ELSIE VENNER. 1868. GUARDIAN ANGEL. 1870. POET AT BREAKFAST TABLE.	1861-66. BIGLOW PAPERS (Second Series). 1865, July 21. COMMEMORATION ODE. 1869. CATHEDRAL.	1862. Death of Thoreau. (Born 1817.) 1863. Lincoln's Gettysburg speech.
	1879. Life of Motley. The Iron Gate.	1872-74. Abroad. 1875-76. THREE MEMORIAL ODES. 1877-80. Minister to Spain.	1878. Death of Bryant. (Born 1794.) 1880. Concord School of Philosophy founded.
1890. Quadrimillennial of Haverhill. Poem by Whittier.	1884. Life of Emerson. 1887. 100 Days in Europe.	1880-85. Minister to England.	1881. J. T. Fields died. (Born 1817.)
†1892, Sept. At Hampton Falls, N.H.	†1894, Oct. In Boston.	†1891, Aug. At Elmwood, Cambridge.	1892. Death of G. W. Curtis. (Born 1824.)

CONTENTS

I

                                                     PAGE

INTRODUCTION (pp. 1–20).

    English Literature in New England . . . 1
    The Group and the Background . . . 10

II

EMERSON (pp. 21–47).

    The Philosophic Poet 21

III

HAWTHORNE (pp. 48–104).

    A Lonely Life 48
    The Earlier Sketches 67
    The Great Romances 82
    Other Works 93
    The Artist's Compensations 96

IV

LONGFELLOW (pp. 105–154).

    The Youth of a Poet 105
    Longfellow's Maturity . . 130

V

WHITTIER (pp. 155–194).

PAGE

    The Quaker Laureate of Puritanism . . . 155

VI

LOWELL (pp. 195–231).

    Poet and Patriot 195
    The Outward Life 204
    The Heart of the Singer 217

VII

HOLMES (pp. 232–254).

    The Last Leaf 232

VIII

RETROSPECT AND PROSPECT (pp. 255–263).

THE NEW ENGLAND POETS

I

INTRODUCTION

English Literature in New England

Literature is an artistic product, as truly as sculpture or architecture. All the fine arts have for their aim perfection of form, the creation of beauty: but, to a Puritan at least, nothing seems permanently beautiful which fails to suggest heroic human endeavor. Artists must, indeed, take their material, and in some degree their suggestions, from their individual and local environment. Yet, of all creative work, the expression of thought in language is least limited by space or time. The Erechtheum is a ruin, and can never leave its desolated Acropolis; the Vatican torso has outlived its proper setting; it stands lost and dethroned in a gallery of antiques; but Homer remains crowned and serene, as clear-voiced as ever, in far higher honor, indeed, than the singer in his lifetime can ever have dreamed of being. Still, *all* the creations of genius are imperishably beautiful. Perhaps their greatest helpfulness to men lies precisely herein, that they lift us, in imagination, quite out of all the cramping limitations besetting our daily routine: out of mere reality into the ideal world.

Possibly no group of creative writers ever fitted more naturally and easily into their setting, than the authors of Concord, Cambridge, and Boston. Yet, while Emerson and his friends will always be known as the New England poets, their origin, their life, their influence, is neither chiefly sectional, nor even merely national. New England did not create them, did not own them, cannot contain them. As truly as that earlier singer, whose time is disputed, whose name is denied, and to whose wide-wandering ghost an earthly abiding-place will doubtless never be granted, so these whom we fondly call our own, are in truth mankind's κτῆμα ἐς ἀεί — a treasure forevermore.

Nor do we turn to them chiefly, or most

confidently, for a better knowledge of New England life. Sir Launfal is at least as precious to many of us as 'Zekiel, or as Hosea himself; Donatello and Miriam outshine the paler pair of our own folk standing beside them. Whittier himself has sung Stonewall Jackson's march through Frederick, and even the relief of far-off Lucknow, more thrillingly — perhaps more truly — than Floyd Ireson's ride!

It has sometimes been proposed, as a graceful tribute to our most popular authors, that their statues should be set up in public parks, surrounded by the ideal beings who are the creatures of their genius. In Longfellow's case this would surely include Hiawatha and his Minnehaha, Evangeline and Gabriel, perhaps also that kingly pair, Robert of Sicily and Olaf the Dane; certainly we could not spare dear Elsie, who offers her young life so gladly for her prince, in the Legenda Aurea. Yet these favorites are almost wholly folk who never could have breathed our air, or understood a word of our speech.

What is so evidently true of this poet, still the dearest to the national heart, is quite as true of the masters in fiction everywhere. Creative authors never merely sketch such an individual man or woman as they, and we, have known. Every true stroke delineates more the universal than the particular. Is Andromache a Grecian, like her minstrel, a Trojan, like her husband, or the Cilician daughter of Eëtion? No one ever cared to ask. She is the type of sorrowing wifehood in the bitter hours of war and bereavement. As in Homer's day, so in ours. Romola, Miriam, and even Lorna are neither living individuals nor racial types. They are merely typical woman-souls. Each is an ideal of nineteenth-century womanhood, but we are made to see, too, how in her, as in us, all the past experience of humanity is crystallized into expression, all serener future possibilities are foreshadowed.

The same test may be safely applied even to the prince of artists. Ophelia has no Danish feature, Juliet is Italian only in her absolute impulsive naturalness: it never occurred to us that Rosalind is a French demoiselle! Neither has the great magician metamorphosed them all into English girls, and assigned them to the Elizabethan age — or to any other generation. They abide in a fairer land than merry England or sunny France, in statelier homes than Veronese palace or royal castle of Denmark: for they dwell lovingly together in the noble realm of art and ideal beauty. That which is most precious, and most lasting, in a poem, a tale, or even an essay, is least distinctively English, or American, or French. It is "Euripides the Human," Montaigne the human, Burns the human, whose influence lives and works long-lasting as the world.

The "Scarlet Letter" has a vivid local setting, — and so has the "Heart of Mid-Lothian." Neither is a masterpiece merely, or chiefly, because it is a more or less accurate study of Puritanism in New England, or of Scottish life. Hawthorne's genius, and perhaps Scott's also, is revealed, rather, in the treatment of that most universal of problems, the vain attempt to escape from the inherent penalty of sin. As Rembrandt throws the high light on human faces, so does every great artist, whatever the material in which he works. Tito is man tempted and fallen; Savonarola, like Romola, is man rising heroic from temptation and from the bewilderment of self-delusion. Indeed, Savonarola's right to appear in the book must be vindicated, if at all, by the part he plays in the central plot of the romance. Whether the real reformer of Florence was just such a man, whether the background is archæologically accurate: these are alike minor details, hardly touching æsthetic criticism at all.

The recent death of our most influential writer reminds us of the question once so fiercely debated, whether "Uncle Tom's Cabin" was a truthful picture of slavery days in Kentucky and Louisiana. If it could be proved that no black family was ever separated, no innocent negro ever flogged, since Jamestown was founded, the swarthy hero of a baseless romance would remain as deathless as Homer's impossible son of the sea-nymph, with his magic armor and his talking horse! Both are truly drawn, since they act in response to the most universal human motives. No other test of artistic quality is essential.

Yet we must once more reverse the shield of

truth. While the artist's thought is thus free and eternal, the form in which he clothes it is largely shaped for him by usage and tradition, even before he himself is born. Phidias, the pupil of his Hellenic masters, working under the Attic sky, was not merely forced to use his native Pentelic marble, instead of New Hampshire granite — or "staff": it was equally impossible, or inconceivable, for him, upon the Acropolis, to rear a Florentine dome or a Gothic spire.

Even so, we who speak and write the English tongue cannot escape — the wise do not even struggle against — the masterful influence of the myriad workers who through so many centuries have moulded and perfected Anglo-Saxon speech. We, and those who form our audience, have been from infancy the pupils of Chaucer (Professor Child would have bidden me say, of Cædmon) and of Tennyson, and of all the goodly array between. Whatever is traditional in all our arts, except perhaps music, is chiefly and primarily English in form, though it is largely Greek in spirit. Moreover, free as the writer is, he, especially, works in materials which have already been shaped for him : even, it may be, moulded over and over before him, by weak hands as well as strong. A really fresh rhyme brings us nowadays almost a shock of surprise. In this matter our mother-tongue, with its excessive variety of endings, gives us rather step-motherly fare. Our *fountains* can never seek their source anywhere save in the familiar *mountains*, their *shadows* are not only compelled to traverse the *meadows*, but to endure the reproach of an imperfect echo even there! We sometimes seem to ourselves almost like those late Romans who shaped their structures wholly out of blocks, ready carved, taken from the earlier buildings.

The "Chicago Dial," especially, has long waged an effective warfare, of argument and ridicule, against the notion, that American literature in general, and sectional Western literature in particular, should cut loose from the English traditions that make up the past, and grow from roots deep-struck in a virginal native soil. It is in fact only very incompletely, if at all, that literature in America can ever tear itself free from the parent stock in what Hawthorne was fond of calling "Our Old Home." It is precisely the vital English element in our language and literature, in our political and social instincts, in our entire civilization indeed, that has enabled us in any hopeful degree to assimilate that chaotic mass of humanity which year by year has poured into the great gateway of Manhattan. The last thing a far-sighted patriot can desire is a weakening of any ties which still bind us to the happiest of our many fatherlands, the island stronghold

> "Where Freedom broadens slowly down
> From precedent to precedent."

May even the exigencies of politics never again require an outburst of half-sincere jealousy, or unreasoning rage, against our next of kin, "such as of late o'er pale Britannia past!" But, at any rate, the sincere student of letters must see clearly that we (I speak now for the "old New Englanders") are twice-transplanted Anglo-Saxon folk, who, in the forms of our speech, as chiefly in the forms of our life, have been moulded by the long, slow centuries of English growth.

And yet, so far as the instinct of the artist awakes in each man, the boundless universe is his. The environment in which he sets his gem, or his cathedral, may be as homely and familiar as Maud Muller's farm: it may be the vaguest spot in "desolate, wind-swept space." One thing only is essential, the presence, or the suggestion, of human beings acting from motives not wholly ignoble, as we ourselves might conceivably act, or wish that we had acted. Even Homer, or Sappho, or Sophocles, can teach us, directly, little more than what Sidney said, and Longfellow only echoed:

"Look, then, into thy heart, and write!"

The Group, and the Background

In attempting, then, the sympathetic study of this group of literary artists, so largely homogeneous in spirit and aims, let us endeavor to keep constantly in mind that they belong, as artists, to universal humanity, while they are, also, by inheritance and tradition, brother-pilgrims of the goodly company that fills all the highways and lanes of English song, from the Tabard Inn of Southwark to the Red Horse in Sudbury.

New England has held the leadership in our literature heretofore, partly, at least, because it remained nearest in every way to the mother-land. If that leadership has now finally passed away, it is largely because the Keltic and Latin invasions have driven so much of the old stock farther west. The social and scholarly traditions of a half-century ago are now preserved, perhaps, almost as much in Michigan or Ohio as in Massachusetts and Connecticut. Instead of New Haven and Cambridge, Ann Arbor and Oberlin may be regarded as the western bulwarks of a newer New England.

All these six were loyal sons of the Northeast. Not one of them would have spurned, or ignored for an instant, the rugged land in whose bosom all of them now lie at rest. In one or two, even the note of provinciality is at times plainly to be heard; whether deliberately and aggressively struck as in Hosea Biglow, or unconsciously as in Whittier: New

England loves them none the less because they speak in their native dialect!

A most pleasing feature is the bond of generous friendship knitting them all together. When the great romancer died, the five poets were all among the band of a dozen personal friends who followed him to his grave at Concord, the white locks of his classmate, Longfellow, leading the little procession. Of each and all the words of Longfellow hold true:

> "He did not find his sleep less sweet
> For music in some neighboring street."

Surely Longfellow's own sleep was the sweeter year after year, indeed, for the knowledge that his younger friend's music in a neighboring street was of a strain at least as pure and lofty as his own. Of the mutual helpfulness and inspiration in such a circle, Dr. Holmes speaks loyally and wisely in the opening paper of the "Autocrat."

There was much besides kindred blood and common environment to draw them together. They were men sound and sane of nature, free from the fever of wild passion, but full of the steadfast Puritan warmth and earnestness of temper.

They were happy and faithful in their domestic relations; indeed, all save Whittier, who never married, owed constant relief, and much of their inspiration, to their devoted and congenial wives. All took a wise measure of their own powers, and did earnestly, but with due economy, the work for which they were best fitted. All met upon such common ground as patriotism, hatred of oppression and slavery, and liberal but fervent religious faith.

The great difficulty a New England man of our generation finds in discussing these poets is, that all his own early associations and interests are permeated and dominated by them. Many of our elementary emotions and everyday thoughts seem always to have expressed themselves in verses of Longfellow and phrases of Emerson. We cannot "hitch our wagon to a star," nor even "think of the beautiful town that is seated by the sea," without them! To analyze them and compare them with other authors, is like criticising our parents' features, or expounding the charm of our native landscape.

The sturdy stock planted upon the northeastern shores of our common country was long too busy with ruder tasks to cultivate the fair flower of imaginative literature. As Emerson says (in "Social Aims"), "The necessity of clearing the forest, laying out town and street, and building every house and barn and fence, then church and townhouse, exhausted such means as the Pilgrims brought, and made the whole population poor; and the like necessity is still found in each new settlement in the Territories." The horrors of Indian wars, and later the struggle against English tyranny, absorbed much of their energies as well.

Then a stern and joyless creed, teaching the utter vileness of lost man, and the retributive severity of the Divinity, must have repressed the happier flights of their imagination. Grim tales of witch and wizard, of phantom ships and evil spirits, they repeated and believed. Credulous old Cotton Mather, who is largely responsible for the witchcraft persecutions, has left behind him a stout volume filled with such marvels.

But only when handed down to a mellower age, and to men of gentler faith, did these become, for a Hawthorne and a Whittier, the plastic materials of romance and poetry. These Magnalia of Cotton Mather, Bradford's and Winthrop's Journals, the Diary of Samuel Sewall, the sermons and the close-linked theological philosophy of Jonathan Edwards, with many other equally ponderous tomes, survive to record the courage, the piety, even the learning of our forefathers; and to make clear that belles-lettres could never have found toleration in their stern, narrow, heroic lives!

The purely literary masterpieces of contemporary England were actually unknown for generations. It is declared by a careful student that there is no trace, down to the year 1700, of any copy existing in New England of either Shakspeare or Milton: though this last statement is so surprising that Mr. Lowell's resolute incredulity ought perhaps to be mentioned, if only as an encouragement to other doubters.

Indeed, it was not in New England that the first literary men of national and international fame appeared. As to Franklin, Philadelphia, his kindlier stepmother, will at least dispute the claims of Boston. In the patriotic and political eloquence of the revolutionary period Virginia had the largest share. Freneau, a few of whose early verses are like the first twittering of half-awakened birds before the dawn, was born in New York. Irving and his friends had little connection with the East. Even Bryant we have not, upon the whole, felt justified in including among New England poets, any more than Poe, though both happen to have been born in Massachusetts: Poe, indeed, by a curious freak of fate, actually in Boston.

But very early in the present century, at latest, Boston was evidently becoming the centre of a deeper and more serious culture than our continent had known,—a culture which was preparing the congenial soil from which a creative literature could spring up. From this cultivation other rich fruits have grown. The historical field, in particular, counts Ticknor, Prescott, Motley, Palfrey, Parkman, and others. Webster, Choate, Sumner, and Phillips are as many marked types of forensic eloquence. Channing and Parker were as magnificently diverse in pulpit oratory as in spirit and temper, while Hedge and Freeman Clarke were their worthy successors. Nor do any of these lists exhaust even the most illustrious names. Yet the popular voice undoubtedly sets forth these six, especially, as the New Englanders with whom every lover of pure literature must be well acquainted, — in the order of their birth, Emerson, Hawthorne, Longfellow, Whittier, Holmes, Lowell.

It can hardly be necessary to apologize for including Hawthorne among the poets. For our present purpose poetry may be defined as imaginative literary creation in artistic form: and to this title, certainly, "The Gray Champion" and "Scarlet Letter" have as unquestioned a claim as the "Commemoration Ode" or "Hiawatha." We perhaps lack a term as wide as the German "Dichtung," to include poetical work unfettered by regular rhythm. Emerson asserts — too broadly, I think — that the Germans account Goldsmith a poet (Dichter), as the author of the "Vicar of Wakefield," not of the "Deserted Village."

To this definition of the literary art as the creation of a beautiful form, the objection may naturally be made that the *matter* is of supreme importance. Both the precept and the example of Emerson often seem to support the famous maxim of grim old Cato, who though not primarily a literary critic, has some earmarks of the tribe:

"Rem tene, verba sequentur."

(Get hold of the matter, the words will come of themselves.)

But there is no real disagreement here. The schoolmaster is quite right in his iteration, "Don't say you understand it but you can't express it!" Utterance is the only human test of comprehension. Clear thinking and clear expression, noble ideas and perfect grace in utterance, are mutually helpful, are indeed but as the obverse and reverse of the same medal. In Lincoln's speech at Gettysburg, in Emerson's hymn, written to be sung "By the rude bridge that arched the flood," in Hawthorne's "Snow Image," who can ever consider the thought and expression separately? Emerson says: "I might even say that the rhyme is there in the theme, thought, and image themselves. Ask the fact for the form. The verse must be alive, and inseparable from its contents."

Emerson's own poetic art, in particular, is indeed often incomplete. His clay seems to stiffen under his hand before he has finished the image. Or to change the figure, we are reminded of a beautiful quartz crystal only half-detached from the rough and opaque rock behind it. Lowell hits this (rather too hard) in the rollicking verses of the " Fable for Critics," *e.g.*:

> " In the worst of his poems are mines of rich matter,
> But thrown in a heap with a crush and a clatter."

There is crudeness of form in Emerson's verse, but hardly much clattering and crushing! These unfinished fragments from an artistic workshop have often a peculiar attractiveness, such as Hawthorne felt in a half-worked statue, still partly imprisoned, as he taught us to feel, within the block where it had so long waited only for the sculptor's releasing hand. But even here, it is the perfected crystal and not the rock, the statue rather than the block of marble, that supplies — of course, with the aid of our imagination — every charm save that of contrast. And while a few such unfinished experiments have seen the light, far more were recast in a more suitable mould, or broken up altogether, and returned to the star-dust of Emersonian thought.

Finally, Emerson would have been the last to claim or see any merit in crudeness or obscurity. Still less would he ever affect tortuous or vague expression for its own sake, as Browning, despite his ringing denial, often seems to do. Though the so-called transcendentalism of Emerson has affected Lowell also at times, the mysticism is wholly in the ideal tendencies of their thought, and never darkens the expression. Perhaps Emerson's calm, strong "*Apologia pro vita sua*," entitled "The Transcendentalist," is as good an illustration as can be offered of both these features: mystical depth of thought and transparent clearness in expression. But we are already past the turning of the leaf.

II

EMERSON

EMERSON THE POET

By seniority of birth, by a self-poised independence in life and art, and by the loyal acknowledgment of his friends, Ralph Waldo Emerson is pointed out unmistakably as the leader in this school of literature. In particular, his oration "The American Scholar," delivered to the Harvard Phi Beta Kappa Society on August 31, 1837, was widely hailed as the "Declaration of Independence for American literature," and exerted a lasting influence upon that whole generation, for which it seemed to usher in a new era.

With him, then, we naturally begin. As with the others, his biography is in itself uneventful. All the six, indeed, were born in modest but respectable surroundings. All were early influenced by the best New England culture. All, save Whittier, were educated at Harvard or Bowdoin College. All lived long tranquil lives, chiefly devoted to literature; and, early or late, every one enjoyed, in his lifetime, the general love and admiration of his countrymen.

Emerson sprang from seven generations of Puritan clergymen. This did not in his case indicate anything narrowing or cramping in the intellectual or spiritual influences which made up his environment. About half the earlier graduates of Harvard College became clergymen: the founders being more successful in this direction than in their other object, the pious education of the Indian youth! (It is said that only *one* little Indian ever carried off his sheepskin from Harvard, — and that even he soon after relapsed to wigwam and blanket!) The Unitarian movement of 1800–1820 had been preparing for at least a half century, and indeed from the early eighteenth century onward there had been constant complaint and suspicion against the too liberal atmosphere of Harvard College. Emerson's father, pastor of the oldest Boston Congregational church till his premature death in 1811, was liberal, not to say radical, in his beliefs, introduced little theology into his sermons, and foreshadowed the gentle tolerance so notable in his son.

From his birth (May 25, 1803) Ralph Waldo Emerson had every encouragement to simple living and lofty, free-ranging thought. The slender income of his widowed mother did not prevent the fullest education of her sons.

Emerson does not express enthusiastic gratitude for inspiration from his academic teachers: yet among his instructors at Harvard were Edward Everett in Greek, and George Ticknor in modern languages. He listened also, in Boston, to the political eloquence of Webster and the sermons of William Ellery Channing, whose writings are still the best exposition of the more conservative Unitarianism, as contrasted with the aggressive radicalism of Theodore Parker. Perhaps the chief among Emerson's direct instructors, however, was another member of that brilliant and fertile stock, — Edward Tyrrel Channing, brother of the preacher. This great educator held the Boylston chair of rhetoric and oratory in Harvard College for more than thirty years (1819–

1851), and the claim is sometimes made for him (by old Harvard men, like E. E. Hale and T. W. Higginson) that his pupils include nearly all the Americans of that generation who ever learned how to write!

After a brief experience in teaching, and a course in divinity, Emerson, in 1829, was ordained as a Unitarian clergyman. This career he abandoned three years later, chiefly because he was unwilling to continue the ceremony of the Communion, which he did not believe to have been intended by the Founder as a permanent Christian rite. His temperate farewell sermon on this subject is extant. The rest of his rather mild pulpit discourses he did not wish preserved.

During a brief visit abroad, in 1833, his friendship with Carlyle began. It continued, with hardly a cloud, throughout their lives. To be sure, the broad Atlantic rolled between. It is too curious to imagine what might have occurred if only domineering Tam had accepted the invitation to come over and edit the "Dial."

Upon Emerson's return, in 1834, he settled in Concord. There he was, for nearly half a century, known and loved by all, and a useful citizen in town meeting and in all local affairs. This settlement in Concord is important in the general story of American literature. With the exception of Hawthorne, the writers and thinkers since associated with that quiet village, *e.g.* Thoreau, Alcott, Margaret Fuller, were drawn thither as disciples or friends of Emerson, and they form about him something more like a literary school than has elsewhere appeared.

In this same year, 1834, Emerson entered the lecture field, and initiated the so-called Transcendental Movement. As he himself reminds us, only the name was (comparatively) new. It was the old appeal from the outward realities of life to the diviner intuitions of the human soul. In a striking passage he shows how in all ages this appeal has been repeated:

"This way of thinking, falling on Roman times, made Stoic philosophers: falling on despotic times, made patriot Catos and Brutuses: falling on superstitious times, made prophets and apostles: on popish times, made protestants and ascetic monks, preachers of Faith against the preachers of Works: on prelatical times, made Puritans and Quakers; and falling on Unitarian and commercial times, makes the peculiar shades of Idealism which we know." This sentence strangely omits the first and most famous of idealists, Plato, to whom much of Emerson's philosophy is a direct reversion.

The Transcendentalist, or, as Emerson would have preferred to be called, the Idealist, insists above all that the material things we call realities are in continual flow and ebb, appearing and vanishing; and are, also, wholly beyond man's control, or even his real knowledge; while heroism, truth, love, justice, and the other abstractions, stigmatized by the commercial spirit as intangible, are alone eternal, unchangeable, within the soul's reach, and precious to man. No one would realize better than Emerson that the theme is no new one; but indeed it is the oldest and most unquestionable truths that need most constant iteration. In pointing men's thoughts away from material things to the everlasting verities, he invokes to his aid every spiritual teacher from the hymns of the Vedas to Swedenborg. But

Emerson's own contribution is larger than his borrowings. In particular, he applies to this end, with that poetic largeness of vision which is the truest accuracy, the latest doctrines of science, *e.g.* the infinite permutations of matter in varying chemical forms, or the convertibility and indestructibility of force. He even anticipates Evolution in various poetic utterances, *e.g.*:

> "And striving to be man, the worm
> Mounts thro' all the spires of form."

Perhaps the most pervading element of all Emerson's work is his optimism. The universe, whether viewed outwardly or as a reflection in man's soul, is in perfect harmony. Evil to him is only negative, — the absence of good, — and must everywhere lose ground and at last disappear. Against the acutest forms of present evil, for instance, slavery, Emerson lifts his voice fearlessly and in unmistakable tones. But he never doubts the complete and swift victory of every righteous cause.

Against the mercantile spirit, the vulgar standards of success as tested by wealth and material prosperity, Emerson echoed the protests uttered by the wiser minds of every age. Such a paper as his upon "Politics" occasionally assumes a sharper tone of reproof, which is unhappily quite as much needed by us of the next generation as by his contemporaries. It was not, however, his chief mission to work effectively in company with other men for practical reforms. Even among the great antislavery leaders he remains somewhat apart, the critic, the philosopher, the observer, standing for those highest ideals toward which present reforms only slowly tend. He did not enter at all into the famous Communistic experiment at Brook Farm, though he was during part of those very years Editor of the "Dial," which was largely the organ of the Roxbury community. Naturally this apparent aloofness brought some severe complaints from those who counted upon him for more direct and practical aid; but he never complained of being "misunderstood." He calmly fulfilled his mission and trusted in God.

This half century of mature life was spent almost wholly in New England, and his brief absences — even a successful lecturing tour in England — had little effect upon his development. Indeed, in a sense he developed little after he passed the half-way house of life. His influence was a steadfast and consistent one, and steadily widened to something as like popularity as an ethical teacher and mystic philosopher could ever hope to attain. His life in Concord, meanwhile, we may describe as one of refined economy, or at least of austerest simplicity. The material accumulated for annual courses of lectures appeared with little change as successive volumes of essays, — of which we now count nine, including posthumous collections.

Still more slowly grew his little volume of poems. These are never the impulsive record of a passing mood or incident. Herein they differ as widely as possible from the verses of his friend Holmes, which are nearly all "occasional." [Each Emersonian poem is, rather, the deliberate, labored, final expression of a calm philosophic thought.] It has not been my purpose to delineate, even in outline, Emerson the religious and social teacher, the philosopher, the scholar; yet these phases are all needed to explain Emerson the artist, the poet. We have so masterly a critic as Lowell upon our side in asserting that this is, after all, his chief function and essential character. When Emerson once expressed a doubt if he could ever write poetry, his friend, Frank Sanborn, said, "Some of us think you can write nothing else." Even in his wisest essays he is oftener lyrical than logical. He illuminates his thought by brilliant images and far-flashing divinations, instead of weaving an unbroken chain of argument. These traits are not, to be sure, equally prominent in all his work, though there is a striking evenness in his utterance, since he always moves serenely in the loftiest and purest realms of thought.

Yet a certain homeliness of metaphor and illustration, as in the teachings of the Platonic Socrates with his "cobblers, and fullers, and midwives," constantly reminds us that Emerson is a shrewd practical Yankee farmer and good neighbor, as well as a Neoplatonic mystic and idealist. Here again we are naturally tempted to quote Lowell, but Whittier's "Last Walk in Autumn" will serve as well:

> "He who might Plato's banquet grace,
> Have I not seen before me sit,
>   And watched his Puritanic face
> With more than Eastern wisdom lit?
>   Shrewd mystic! Who upon the back
> Of his Poor Richard's Almanack
>   Writing the Sufi's song, the Gentoo's dream,
> Links Menu's age of thought with Fulton's age of steam!"

This double nature the very face of Emerson reveals even to the most casual student of physiognomy.

Some of Emerson's writings, naturally enough, have little or nothing of mysticism; and in these his clear nervous style and masterly vocabulary give him great power over any reader. This is illustrated especially by his plain unvarnished account of San Domingo slavery, in the Emancipation Address. Of his entire volumes, "English Traits" is possibly the easiest reading, and is perhaps the most searching analysis of England's folk and life that has ever been made. Any one who will read Emerson's discussion of manners in the little paper on "Social Aims," will find himself compelled to take the sermon to heart, and mend his own manners as he may.

Emerson as he grew older fused the two diverse elements of his nature, his practical and ideal sides, more and more fully. There is a popular story, that a friend of President Lincoln once asked him the quizzical question, "Mr. Lincoln, how long do you think a man's legs ought to be?" The great Emancipator, who was rarely caught off his guard in a contest of native wit, replied without hesitation that he had never given the subject careful thought, but it seemed to him — glancing at his own protracted and awkward extremities — that "they ought to be just about long enough to reach the ground." Emerson, without ever withdrawing his head from the loftiest ether, did plant his feet more firmly, with the years, upon his native earth. Certainly I for one confess that his earliest book, "Nature," and some other papers, "The Oversoul," "Circles," etc., are intelligible to me only in very moderate amounts, and only when the reader and his author are in fully sympathetic mood. But in, for example, the later volume, "Letters and Social Aims," or the paper entitled "Wealth," in the "Conduct of Life," much the same subjects are treated quite as loftily and rigorously; yet the more cogent linking of the reasoning, the richer illustration, perhaps the greater clearness and maturity of Emerson's own thought and style, carry us along as it were despite ourselves, and command full attention to the end. Many more young people would learn to love and crave Emerson if set to read the first paper in the volume just referred to, "Poetry and Imagination," lofty and wide-reaching as it is, than if their introduction to the philosopher were through the thin volume entitled "Nature," which in his early youth won him "fit audience though few." A well-known poem, "The Apology," has the lines:

> "I go to the god of the wood
> To fetch his word to men."

In this first prose work Emerson seems hardly yet to have relearned fully the speech, and recalled the interests, of his kind, after a longer and deeper forest-seclusion than was his later wont.

Inadequate as is this bird's-eye view of the general life and work of Emerson, we must hasten on, to touch upon a few favorites among the poems, into which his purest thoughts are crystallized. Of this preëminence of poetry, Emerson himself often assures us. "Poetry is the consolation of mortal men. They live, 'cabined, cribbed, confined,' in a narrow and trivial lot . . . A poet comes who lifts the veil; gives them glimpses of the laws of the universe . . ." Indeed, in the closing strain of "Poetry and Imagination" he almost seems to echo Clough's thought in "Come, Poet, Come!" viz., that the end and object of human life itself is to furnish fit material for the poet! Emerson's words are, "Sooner or later that which is now life shall be poetry, and every fair and manly trait shall add a richer strain to the song."

That perfect harmony through all outward nature, which is the essence of beauty, he has indicated in a very familiar poem, "Each and All": perhaps his best example of finished form. The poem has an absolutely perfect unity and simplicity; it expresses fully its lofty lesson, yet there is scarcely a violent rhyme, a verse that will not scan, still less a sentence that will not parse, in its fifty lines, all enforcing the truth, "Nothing is fair or good alone." This poem all should know by heart.

Nearly the same thought occurs often in Emerson. Thus it flashes out in a glorious image, set to a strain of immortal music, in the midst of one longer poem, much of which moves in an air rather too remote and attenuated for most of us to breathe: I mean the second part of "Woodnotes." The verses were, I think, selected by Bayard Taylor in his clever "Echo Club" as the sweetest of all Emersonian strains:

> "For Nature beats in perfect tune,
>   And rounds with rhyme her every rune . . .
>   Thou canst not wave thy staff in air,
>   Or dip thy paddle in the lake,
>   But it carves the bow of beauty there,
>   And the ripples in rhyme the oar forsake."

Almost as famous as "Each and All" is the "Problem." But here many readers are disposed to strip off like a husk the outer setting and nominal subject, to seize merely the illustrations, which are themselves a series of miniature lyrics. Especially beautiful is the reminder, how great works of art, harmonizing perfectly with the natural scenery in which they are set, become themselves a part of nature's perfection. The lesson is enforced by a series of noble figures:

> "Earth proudly wears the Parthenon
> As the best gem upon her zone;
> And Morning opes with haste her lids
> To gaze upon the Pyramids.
> O'er England's abbeys bends the sky,
> As on its friends with kindred eye.
> For out of thought's interior sphere
> These wonders rose to upper air;
> And Nature gladly gave them place,
> Adopted them into her race,
> And granted them an equal date
> With Andes and with Ararat."

(The last line may seem wilful, but it is by no means Emerson's boldest venture. He forces rhyme to his needs with all Dante's ruthlessness. It requires the Puritan's calm courage to cap *bear* with *woodpecker*, as he does in "Woodnotes"!)

The fleeting nature of what we call property, the folly of mortal man who says of the earth "It is mine," are set forth with resistless force in a tranquil lyric, which Emerson has dared to begin with a mere string of Concord family names: following strangely upon the mystic Oriental title "Hamatreya."

> "Bulkely, Hunt, Willard, Hosmer, Merriam, Flint,
> Possessed the land."

We shiver, as at the tread upon our own graves, when the same slow music glides fearlessly on into the tragic truth of life:

> "*Where are these men?* Asleep beneath their grounds,
> And strangers, fond as they, their furrows plough.
> Earth laughs in flowers, to see her boastful boys,
> Earth-proud, proud of the earth which is not theirs;
> Who steer the plough, but cannot steer their feet
> Clear of the Grave."

"The Snowstorm" is the least ethical or significant of the poems: hardly more than a picture. But as such it almost rivals "Snowbound" itself, though counting little more than a score of quiet verses. We are tempted to question how often, in any climate,

> "Announced by all the trumpets of the sky
> Arrives the snow,"

but it may have been so in 1834. Mr. Emerson has not given such copious proof of his accurate observation out-of-doors as Mr. Lowell and Colonel Higginson: though even here "May-Day," and other passages, may well give us pause.

The brief poem "Rhodora" is a deep lesson in seemingly artless art. Beginning with a reminiscent picture, and gliding into a fancied conversation, it leaves the sting of a great truth in our memory and is gone "ere we are aware!"

The relation of Emerson's verse to his prose may be illustrated by such poems as "Compensation," which has condensed into eight lines, and crystallized there in a single image, the essential lesson of the famous essay bearing the same title. And we may add that the verses win a complete and unquestioning acceptance; while the essay, in part at least, affects many readers as a beautiful, impressive, noble web of sophistical special pleading. Similarly, his code of manners is wonderfully packed into the eight lines called "Forbearance"; though this masterpiece does not indeed make less indispensable the fuller teachings in "Social Aims." That he can elaborate an Elizabethan "conceit," even, as happily as Herrick, though not without touching it with a deeper tenderness, is proved by the "Amulet." The next poem, "Thine Eyes still Shined," seems to a lover of Goethe's "Ich denke Dein" more like a literary echo than anything else in the volume.

Of the merely personal or subjective element, often too prominent in the lyric poet, we rarely have even a hint in Emerson. Of his brothers, two of whom, at least, but for their premature death, would have shared largely in his spirit, his influence, and his fame, he speaks tenderly in the "Dirge." But neither the rhythmic movement nor the lyric unity are noticeably strong here, and perhaps only the two closing lines will live:

> "The silent organ loudest chants
> The master's requiem."

"Threnody," indeed, one of the most perfect among the longer poems, has a tenderly personal side, being occasioned by the death of Emerson's child, a wonderfully precocious boy. It is in part, too, a vividly realistic picture of the beloved son's life. But the father's grief, like Tennyson's sorrow for his friend, Arthur Hallam, is but the occasion from which the poet's thoughts rise to the theme, accounted of men the loftiest and weightiest of all: the assurance of immortality. Through lighter thoughts, and more jocund pictures, a still longer poem, "May-Day," circles upward to the same clear final note of confident hope:

"Through earth to ripen, through Heaven endure."

Among his briefer lyrics, at least, Emerson's own favorite was "Days." As to the yet more famous "Brahma," he seems to have been more amused than wounded by the ridicule and rather coarse banter with which this pearl of mystic truth was received, when it appeared in the first number of the "Atlantic Monthly." The key to nearly all its difficulties is in the title, which should remind us that it is not the poet that speaks, but the all-pervasive, indestructible Spirit Divine. Pantheism appealed strongly to Emerson. That Longfellow also felt the charm of the same mystical faith, may be seen from a beautiful interlude of the "Wayside Inn":

"It was his faith, perhaps is mine,
That life in all its forms is one."

Among other poems perfectly intelligible and enjoyable for any lover of verse are "Good-by,"

"The Humble-bee" (which owes something, as Hawthorne hinted, in his "Virtuoso's Collection," to the Anacreontic apostrophe to the Cicada), the first "Woodnotes," and "Adirondacks": a poem that Stillman, the leader of the actual excursion, has recently discussed in a notable paper. There is just a glorifying tinge of mysticism in "Waldeinsamkeit" and "Two Rivers." But our list must not grow to a catalogue. Is it not Lowell who somewhere says, that we will thank him who points out the brook to us, but he need not catch us the trout? I need only assure the seeker that Emerson's slender rill, cold and clear from loftiest Parnassus, teems with shy beauties only waiting to be caught.

Much of Emerson's poetic material never crystallized into coherent verse at all. A little was suppressed as unworthy, even after publication, and not without reason. Since his death, quite a mass of fragments, found among his papers, has been printed with his poems. Here we find, for instance, "disjecta membra," large and small, of a poem on "The Poet," at which Emerson labored at intervals for more than twenty years; yet it never took shape. It is instructive to study these bits, as it is to examine the memoranda in Hawthorne's American Notebooks, whether they were or were not successfully elaborated into tales in his later life. Occasionally a couplet or quatrain of these verses is as perfect as the best epigrams in the Greek Anthology. For instance, any man who wanders, in bereavement or disheartenment, under the midnight sky, may be glad to have Emerson voice his feeling for him:

> "Teach me your mood, O patient stars,
> Who climb each night the ancient sky,
> Leaving on space no shade, no scars,
> No hate of age, no fear to die."

Certainly, if he had a larger design into which such perfectly carved details could have fitted like metopes of a finished Greek temple, we may well regret that he never raised its walls.

But like every true poet, Emerson was conscious that there was much poetry in his soul too lofty, or of too ethereal essence, for utterance in words. There is a beautiful acknowledgment of this in his "Forerunners." Each of our New England poets has expressed this same consciousness. Whittier's "The Vanishers," Lowell's "Envoi To the Muse," a part of Holmes' "The Voiceless," are remarkably close parallels with the "Forerunners." In "Prometheus," the "Wind over the Chimney," and elsewhere, Longfellow has felt — perhaps less deeply — that he, too, had rich treasures of inspiration which could never take form in uttered words.

The present writer has a single far remembrance, from his own boyhood, of Emerson as a lecturer upon "Eloquence" before the New England "Lyceum." The dry, silent smile with which the lecturer confessed his sense of incongruity between his theme and his delivery is still vividly recalled. Indeed, the deliberate half-dreamy utterance, the abstracted manner, the quiet tones of Emerson's old age, were not then as impressive, for boyish listeners, as the shallower, noisier oratory of the war-period. But, especially in smaller audiences of maturer hearers, he was throughout his long life sure of an eager and affectionate hearing. Lowell says, in his reverently critical paper upon "Emerson the Lecturer" (pp. 383-4): "How artfully (for Emerson is a long-studied artist in these things) does the deliberate utterance, that seems waiting for the fit word, appear to admit us partners in the labor of thought, and make us feel as if the glance of humor were a sudden suggestion, as if the perfect phrase — lying written there on the desk — were as unexpected to him as to us." The whole passage — indeed, the whole essay — should be read with care.

Emerson's tranquil old age was characterized by a gradual failing of the memory, and finally by a form of *aphasia*, which limited greatly his power of communication with other men. But the grace of outward manner, and the perfect refinement of his inner nature, could never deteriorate. Indeed it often seemed as if the soul within still mused on themes as lofty as of old, and only the bodily organs declined to transfuse thought into articulate speech.

He was present, in the body, at Longfellow's funeral, and once whispered to his companion, "Who is the sleeper?" But his real self awoke at nightfall, fully conscious that he had lost the day. Just one month later his own frame was at rest.

At an earlier stage of life, when the first consciousness of lessening force admonished him, he composed the lines entitled "Terminus":

> "It is time to be old,
> To take in sail."

He does not overstate here the preciousness of age (as Cicero's extravagant eulogium in the "De Senectute" outbids Plato's moderate words on old age in the "Republic"), nor say with Browning:

> "Grow old along with me;
> The best is yet to be;
> The last of life for which the first was made."

Rather it is the cheerful resignation of Longfellow's "Morituri Salutamus" that we hear in Emerson's lines:

> "As a bird trims her to the gale,
>   I trim myself to the storm of time;
> I man the rudder, reef the sail,
>   Obey the voice at eve obeyed at prime."

This last line Mr. Lowell once used most gracefully, applying it to himself as Mr. Emerson's disciple of thirty years. "I at least," he says, "gladly

"'Obey the voice at eve obeyed at prime.'"

Even the slow and painless decay of Emerson's mind, before the body's dissolution, can give no touch of the tragic to a life so tranquil and content, so full and rounded. There is no baffling of fond hopes, no rich promise unfulfilled, as when Catullus or Keats perishes untimely, or Poe and De Musset squander the rare gifts of genius. His message was fully and even repeatedly delivered: a message indeed of sweetness and light, of unquestioning trust and faith. His art has stimulated many disciples, whether direct imitators, as even fiery-hearted Helen Hunt so often is, or strong masculine souls, like Lowell, that thank him rather for the bugle note of encouragement than for direct aid and suggestion.

But the divine spirit of gentle peace and loving faith abiding in the man is even better than any direct teachings in his books. We of to-day find it simply impossible to imagine what the spiritual air of New England was before Emerson breathed his message and lived his life.

III

HAWTHORNE

A Lonely Life

There is a famous saying of Dr. Holmes', which unites the wit of the man and the physician's wisdom, to the effect that a child's education should begin a hundred years before his own birth. The artistic triumph of Hawthorne came, with a certain suddenness, when the "Scarlet Letter" appeared in 1850. The romancer was then already past middle age, and had been at times disposed to regard himself as hopelessly belated, and foredoomed to failure. Yet it is doubtless generally felt that that book stands alone, by its originality of form, artistic completeness, and deep insight into human nature, at the summit of our national literature. And not merely the solitary youth-time of the author himself, but the conditions of Salem society and his immediate ancestry through two centuries, are clearly seen to have aided in perfecting this late-blooming, deep-hearted flower of imagination, that graces the sombre, crumbling wall of New England Puritanism.

A partial consciousness of cause for gratitude to the past glimmers upon the pages of the famous introduction to the "Scarlet Letter." The frankness of such self-confession by Hawthorne is, to be sure, always elusive. He slips off merely an outer mask, while the artist, at least, if not the man, still conceals his real features only the more effectively. There is no suspicion of a smile, however, behind such sentences as these:

"I seem to have a stronger claim to a residence here (*i.e.* in Salem) on account of this grave-bearded, sable-cloaked, and steeple-crowned progenitor, — who came so early, with his Bible and his sword, and trode the unworn street with so stately a port. . . . He was a soldier, legislator, judge; he was a ruler in the church; he had all the Puritanic traits, both good and evil." Then, after touching on the cruelty shown toward the Quakers by this first Hathorne of Salem, he continues: "His son, too, inherited

E

the persecuting spirit, and made himself so conspicuous in the martyrdom of the witches, that their blood may fairly be said to have left a stain upon him. So deep a stain, indeed, that his old, dry bones in the Charter Street burial-ground must still retain it, if they have not crumbled utterly to dust!" The next sentence, expressing the fear that these earliest ancestors, if unrepentant for their cruelties, may be "now groaning under the heavy consequences of them, in another state of being," is like a glimpse at that cornice of Dante's Purgatorial mount where Pride is atoned. And surely there is no hint of aught but the deepest earnest in the closing words: "At all events I, as their representative, hereby take shame upon me for their sakes, and pray that any curse incurred by them, as I have heard, and as the dreary and unprosperous condition of the race, for many a long year back, would argue to exist, may be now and henceforth removed."

This ancestral curse seems to have been in some sort a matter of family pride; or, at least, was accepted with a consciousness that it could only cling to an ancient and masterful lineage:

as the loyal old Keltic servant silenced the fears of the upstart family that had purchased the ancestral castle of her masters, "Did ye think the Banshee would howl for the likes of *yez?*" The creator of the ill-fated Pyncheons, in the "House of the Seven Gables," plainly borrows largely from his own memories and household traditions. The belief in the inherited ban, doubtless, really aided in perpetuating the self-centred, companionless, silent tendencies of the Hawthornes. The romancer's immediate ancestry for several generations had been mariners, in peace or war; and the life of a sea captain is preëminently a lonely, independent, and uncompanionable existence. Nathaniel Hawthorne evidently felt that the occupancy of one home, and doubtless "inbreeding," too, in Salem, had continued too long for the good of his race; and he made a life-long effort to widen his own horizon.

Hawthorne was born in 1804. His father, a taciturn, book-loving sailor, died abroad when Nathaniel was but four years old. The widow never laid aside her mourning, nor resumed any save the most necessary intercourse with the outside world in the forty remaining years of her life. Much of the boy's childhood was spent under an uncle's roof in Maine, on the wild shores of Sebago Lake. Roaming the woods in summer with his gun, or skimming up and down the frozen lake for lonely miles in winter, he there first acquired if it was not inborn his lifelong delight in solitude. A prolonged lameness, which threatened to become permanent, confirmed in the boy a fondness for reading, especially of romances and poetry, which the mother had never discouraged. Indeed, the mother of a restless boy, who discourages his habit of reading, is yet to be discovered. "Pilgrim's Progress" was a lifelong favorite, and perhaps the one book whose pervasive influence can be traced in Hawthorne's mature work.

At Bowdoin College the personal intercourse between students on the one side, and the instructors, their families, and Brunswick society generally on the other, has always been of the slightest. The diversions of the sturdy, rudely trained Maine youths among themselves can hardly have appealed strongly to the more sensitive city-bred lad. Once, indeed, he is fined and under censure, with other students, for social wine-drinking and card-playing. But here again, as in recalling his boyhood, his most vivid and happy college memories are of long rambles through the pine forests of Maine. His studies did not arouse any craving for the higher scholarship, nor even for collegiate honors. Indeed, the well-known distinction of so many Bowdoin graduates has been, I think, chiefly in other than purely scholastic careers. However, the rather motley collection of books in the college library encouraged his early fondness for desultory reading. Miss Peabody states that, in the little coterie where he was best beloved, Hawthorne, by his personal beauty, his shyness, and his fondness for romantic story-telling, won the pet name of Oberon. This was, at any rate, one of several signatures under which he later dispersed and hid his literary fame. Hawthorne's classmate Bridge says the romancer himself chose the name in those after years.

A quarter century later he writes to Bridge,

in dedicating to him the "Snow Image": "I know not whence your faith came; but while we were lads together at a country college, — gathering blueberries, in study-hours, under those tall academic pines; or watching the great logs as they tumbled along the current of the Androscoggin; . . . or catching trouts in that shadowy little stream which, I suppose, is still wandering riverward through the forest, though you and I will never cast a line in it again, — two idle lads, in short, . . . doing a hundred things that the Faculty never heard of, or else it had been the worse for us, — still it was your prognostic of your friend's destiny that he was to be a writer of fiction." This single, gracefully intertwined sentence — which I have even now abbreviated — illustrates charmingly several Hawthornesque traits; his tenderness in friendship, his half-whimsical self-depreciation, his lingering affection for past associations; but, no less, his skill in detailed word-painting, his unerring choice of the most vivid expression, and that final indescribable touch of tender grace that marks each sentence of his as an artist's own.

But at the college gate Hawthorne parted for long years even from these comrades of what most men call their four happiest years. After graduation in 1825, returning to the silent, unsocial shelter of the Salem roof-tree, he became for the next eight or ten years more and more hermit-like in his daily routine, for weeks together exchanging hardly a word even with the mother and the two sisters who shared the home with him.

There has been, however, an exaggerated and distorted impression as to this period of seclusion in Hawthorne's life. In the first place, he was an athletic and perfectly healthy young man, delighting in long tramps, swimming, and vigorous exercise generally. He was an assiduous student, as a few of his writings directly reveal. "The Virtuoso's Collection," in particular, throws much curious light on Hawthorne's literary byways.

In these years, also, his perfect literary style was created. We hardly needed Hawthorne's own statement that this had cost him long effort: and wide reading is as essential thereto as careful writing. His further remark, that he aimed only at the simplest and most direct expression of his thought, is also undoubtedly true, but most misleading to one who fails to remember how subtle, many-tinted, and evanescent a fanciful Hawthornesque thought could be!

During these years Hawthorne held quite aloof from ordinary social life; for which, indeed, he never had leisure or inclination. He was long debarred, also, from foreign travel, from such stimulating companionship as Cambridge or Concord might have offered him, and even to a great degree from his old intimate friends. But we know, from his American Notebooks and other sources, that he occasionally made prolonged journeys, or tours of observation, and that he was, both then and while at home in Salem, a close student, an interested Spectator (to use the Addisonian word) of the ordinary outward life about him. He says, self-depreciatingly, to Longfellow, that he had had a few glimpses at real life through a peep-hole, and these had occasioned the most successful of his productions. But, to the keen receptive eye of a

Hawthorne, more life and truth came through such a peep-hole than ever reaches most men in the broad daylight of the city street!

"In this dismal chamber," as he wrote in his Notebooks long afterward, "fame was won!" The divine spark of life, of genius, no study in evolution has yet explained. Hawthorne's nature was pure, earnest, strong, and devoted. The conditions, the environment, we can now see, were favorable. The kindling flash is always a miracle from on high!

The growth of Hawthorne's reputation as an author was undoubtedly slow. It is more than a jest when he claims to have been for many years the obscurest writer in America. The conditions were most unfavorable for the prompt recognition of a modest and sensitive author. In fiction, especially, a rhetorical sentimentality pervaded the dominant school, of which N. P. Willis was the best representative (and "Maria dell' Occidente," perhaps, one of the worst). The reading public was slow to acquire a purer taste, if, indeed, the best work is even yet absolutely popular. The old-fashioned Annuals and short-lived literary magazines offered scanty returns in money or reputation. But Hawthorne's various *noms de plume*, and anonymous publication, had also a large share in obscuring his fame. Some, at least, of his youthful works were widely appreciated, before his name was known at all. Thus in one early Annual *four*, unsigned stories of his appeared, not avowedly from the same hand, and all were warmly praised by an English reviewer, — probably Chorley, who afterward knew and loved the writer.

When in 1837 Elizabeth Peabody, with characteristic energy, set out to discover the writer of the sketches that had delighted her in the "New England Magazine," it was with great difficulty that she found they had been written in her own town of Salem, — that they were from the hand of a certain young Hawthorne, — and, finally, that the Hawthorne in question could be no other than a half-forgotten playmate of her childhood. So, when he asks Bridge, "Was there ever such a weary delay in obtaining the slightest recognition from the public as in my case?" we must remember, too, that he had eluded such recognition almost as coyly as he afterward avoided the best social life England could offer him, and had little right to indulge, even half-jestingly, in querulousness as to either literary or personal recognition.

The Peabodys seem to have been literally the only people with whom the Hawthornes had social relations, and it is no wonder if the invalid younger sister, Sophia Peabody, a woman of many gifts, artist, linguist, authoress, and above all, as a sympathetic critic, became almost instantly indispensable to him. Never was love at first sight more fully justified by a lifetime of happiness and mutual helpfulness. In this same year, also, the first series of "Twicetold Tales" appeared in book form. Bridge, without Hawthorne's knowledge, had guaranteed the timid publisher against loss upon the venture. Profit there seems to have been none for many years. Still, this marks an important turn in Hawthorne's life. Within that circle whose opinions he valued his position was at once fixed. Longfellow, in particular, wrote an enthusiastic review of his classmate's book, and made efforts to draw him again into congenial personal relations.

From George Bancroft, then Collector of the Port of Boston, Hawthorne received in 1839 an appointment there as gauger and weigher. This he filled faithfully until turned out, in due routine, by the Whigs, in 1841. These years were brightened by his friendship with Hillard and others, by the slow growth of his literary fame, above all, by the constant and appreciative sympathy of Sophia Peabody. He had now, with the incentive of his troth-plight, saved a thousand dollars; but poverty, the lady's delicate health, and also, possibly, Hawthorne's deference to the supposed wishes of his mother, still delayed their marriage.

Hawthorne now embarked in the famous Brook Farm experiment of transcendental semi-communism, putting into the venture his hard-earned dollars, which he apparently never regained. The next spring he was looking for a suitable site on the Farm to build a cottage for his bride, — when on a sudden impulse he flung down his hoe, and turned his back on the Roxbury community forever. There seems to have been no adequate cause at the moment. We may fancy Margaret Fuller's dominance within-doors during her frequent visits, and work in the fields, hard enough to stifle all artistic creativeness, had slowly filled the cup of discontent, until it now quietly ran over. We certainly cannot regret an experience to which we clearly owe the "Blithedale Romance." In that book is enough autobiographic confession to explain his departure. The most whimsically surprising thing is that he tarried and toiled a year. There is one delicious backward glimpse from his next abode. "It has been an apophthegm these five thousand years, that toil sweetens the bread it earns. For my part (speaking from hard experience, acquired while belaboring the rugged furrows of Brook Farm), I relish best the free gifts of Providence." (Preface to the "Mosses from an Old Manse.")

In 1842 the second collection of "Twicetold Tales" was gathered up from forgotten magazines and published. Miss Peabody's long years of invalidism were ended. Love worked a prompter and completer miracle for the Hawthornes than for the Brownings. Encouraged by an appointment as editor, — which presently failed him, — Hawthorne married in 1842, and settled in the old Manse at Concord, so perfectly described in the introduction to the "Mosses." Here the happy young couple remained, swaying between simple comfort and absolute poverty, for three years. To their daughter Rose we are recently indebted for a delightful picture of "Hyperion," living contentedly as a vegetarian, perforce, on the products of his own garden, and on berries from the neighboring fields, and performing all the drudgery of the kitchen with imperial grace, while his wife held the new-born baby, and directed the tasks she was forbidden to share! There is no purer or quainter picture in the annals of genius.

Hawthorne's second experience in political office-holding was as surveyor in the custom house of his native city, from 1846–1849. The Introduction of the "Scarlet Letter" has given an unwelcome immortality to his associates therein; and in the case of the "Old Inspector," certainly, the artist's enjoyment in the portrayal made him unduly forgetful as to the natural sensitiveness of a live human subject. Even more than at Brook Farm, this daily mechanical employment deadened for the time Hawthorne's artistic existence. His dismissal, in 1849, occurred under exasperating conditions, and plunged him into distress and even lasting debt. But the blow was hailed joyfully by his wife with the words, "Now you can write your book!" The "Scarlet Letter," begun that very day, was indeed completed before they left Salem early in the next year. His mother's painful last illness and death, sickness for himself and all his family, poverty, indebtedness, the slanders against his character circulated to excuse his removal from office, all darkened that eventful winter! The other work of American fiction which would be most generally accounted the rival of the "Scarlet Letter," "Uncle Tom's Cabin," was written a year or two later, piecemeal, beside the evening lamp, by a tired and busy mother, surrounded by the noisy circle of her children. So unconquerably does genius rise superior to untoward conditions!

The discovery of an actual scarlet letter, or of papers explaining its history, in the custom house attic, is a fiction. But in a deeper sense, as we hail this new creation upon a far larger plan than of old, we may really feel that we owe the book, in part, to those years of repression and silence. The stream was only dammed and deepened: it could not be choked.

The actual composition of the "Scarlet Letter" was remarkably rapid. When the Hawthornes left Salem for Lenox, early in 1850, the book had appeared, and had been at once recognized, both at home and in Europe, as a masterpiece. Fame had come, and worldly independence was assured. The next few years, despite three migrations in search of a home, were marked by happy and easy production. "The House of the Seven Gables" and "Wonderbook" were written in Lenox; the "Blithedale Romance" in West Newton; but already in June, 1852, Hawthorne had purchased and moved into Alcott's house, "The

Wayside," in Concord. From "The Wayside" were sent forth only the "Tanglewood Tales" and the "Life of Franklin Pierce."

These changes of abode may perhaps have proved in one respect an aid to the romancer's art. It is worth noticing that in each of his large works he required, after the closest local study, the hazier perspective of distance, both in time and space. The "Scarlet Letter," whose scene is laid in Boston, took shape in Salem, long after his two years of Bostonian life. The Salem story, in turn, was written when the Hawthornes were in Lenox. The Brook Farm experience deadened his literary impulses at the time, and the "Blithedale Romance" was sent forth, ten years later, from a very different home. Even the "Marble Faun" was not written chiefly in Italy, but under the gray English skies.

Upon the accession of Pierce to the Presidency, Hawthorne was offered the lucrative consulship at Liverpool. Here he spent four years, a blank in his literary life, except for the confidential English notebooks. To the two years following, passed in Italy, is due, at

F

least, the outward form of his last masterpiece, the "Marble Faun," though it was not written until 1859-1860. The distressing illness of his daughter Una, at Rome, during 1858, undermined Hawthorne's own constitution, and the four years of declining health at home, 1860-1864, brought the early end of his life-story. These last years were chiefly occupied with uncompleted experiments which were really variations upon one theme, — the "Elixir of Life."

His wife survived him by ten years. His only son is by some critics, notably by R. H. Stoddard, set nearly at the head of living romancers. Una, his well-beloved eldest child, died soon after him; the youngest has lived to become the wife — now the widow — of an American man of letters.

Hawthorne satisfied Solon's conditions of a happy life, and died painlessly, with no previous break in his own family circle, and in the full splendor of his fame. It is the belief of his most admiring and sympathetic critics, that his later works, even if completed, would not have surpassed his finished masterpieces, nor shown a material widening of his scope. Compared with the long and tranquil old age of Whittier and Holmes, his life seems brief, and his death untimely: yet each career has a completeness and harmony of its own. But it is time to turn altogether to the more important side of Hawthorne's life, — his artistic activity.

THE EARLIER SKETCHES

Some poetic and creative writers hardly appear to have a development at all. Thus Bryant wrote two poems in his boyhood, which the man of eighty had never surpassed; nor did his tones ever undergo an essential change. Hawthorne's art evidently had a very deliberate, orderly process of growth. Unhappily the materials for tracing that growth are to some extent lost, and in large degree confused.

His sister has preserved some verses written by him at sixteen. They have the aimless mock-melancholy, and the effort to describe nature without real study of her, that so often characterize boyish poetry.

> "The wind sighs through the trees around,
> And the leaves send forth a gentle sound,
> Like the voices of a dream."

From very similar beginnings, Longfellow's real poetic powers developed; but in Hawthorne such experiments only indicate early attention to the sound of words and the graces of style. (For music, curiously enough, he, like Emerson, never had any adequate appreciation or ear.) In other fragments, preserved in his letters, he is less earnest. A serial paper, edited chiefly for the eyes of his sisters, has some keen flashes of humor from the boy's pen that prove the ancient adage true, by foreshadowing the man's deeper yet gentle irony.

As a student in college, Hawthorne wrote "Seven Tales of my Native Land," and after making serious efforts to have them published, burned them in a fit of despondency. These, if preserved, would probably have shown a kinship to Poe's more grewsome stories. Probably all that was valuable was remembered and utilized again in stories still surviving. Three years later, in 1828, his romance "Fanshawe" was actually printed, and a few copies sold. It is rather gracefully written, slight and unnatural in plot, and vague in characterization. The realistic glimpses of Bowdoin are pleasing, but it is not in any respect an important piece of work. Nathaniel Hawthorne at twenty-four was distinctly inferior in force to Marion Crawford,—not to mention prodigies like Barrie or Kipling. The greatest artists are perhaps oftener not precocious.

From this period onward, until past his fortieth year, we have really a single large stage of Hawthorne's development, represented by the short sketches, essays, and stories collected in the two volumes of "Twicetold Tales," the "Mosses," and the "Snow Image." These are not arranged, chronologically or otherwise. No one of the four volumes is either homogeneous in itself, or clearly distinguishable from the rest. Each gleaning went far back, and included some of his earliest publications. The preface to the "Snow Image," in 1851, finally declares that this volume includes everything of the kind worth preserving, and that there will be no more. Hawthorne had then, indeed, already acquired the full mastery of a larger style. The great romances were taking shape in rapid succession.

It is doubtful whether the works of this period ever can be restored to the true order of their creation. Even when the date of original publication is known, the author may have had the story, not merely growing under his hand, but lying uncalled-for in his desk for years previous. Julian Hawthorne's additions to the published American Notes ("Nathaniel Hawthorne and his Wife," I, pp. 488–505) offer no dates, and only show that the complete and dated volumes of this precious journal, properly edited and published, might often enable us to trace the genesis of a completed work, from the first germ of the romancer's fancy. While so much has been made public of the private life which Nathaniel Hawthorne would have screened from our too curious eyes, this essential service to our greatest literary character has never been duly rendered. We do not know, even, to just what extent the authentic materials exist for a history of his artistic growth. A mere rearrangement of these eighty pieces in the true order of their creation would be of great value, for they have little in common, save a translucent style, and a certain artistic completeness within narrow limits.

It seems important, thus early in our analysis, to insist upon an essential truth, — that the artist is a moral teacher, though he is a very imperfect artist if his pictures need a dogmatic sermon attached, to point out or enforce their lesson! He creates beauty, indeed, but beauty so true to our own ideal nature that it shall inevitably lift our hearts upward toward its own purer realm. This fundamental canon would perhaps exclude altogether from a place among the permanent fruits of Hawthorne's genius a few stories like "Mrs. Bullfrog" and "Mr. Higginbotham's Catastrophe." Though they have a rough plot, yet they seem cruder by far than the mere sketches to be mentioned presently, and indicate that Hawthorne's cleverness in narration antedated the growth of his artistic morality. The unpleasant melodrama of "John Inglefield's Thanksgiving," the crude incompleteness of "Sylph Etheredge," even the excessively tragic atonement in "Roger Malvin's Burial," appear to mark them also as early work, of a time when Hawthorne was still groping toward the moral and æsthetic laws that must guide his art.

In each collection, again, there are some sketches of actual experience, or even of natural scenery, which might well be mere "studies," cut bodily out from the pages of the American Notebooks: studies for backgrounds, we may call them. Such are the "Sights from a Steeple," "Sketches from Memory," "Footprints on the Seashore," "Old Ticonderoga." They are of value, like the Notebooks themselves, chiefly as proof that our first great creative writer was no vague dreamy impressionist, but taught his hand by yearlong practice to set down in the fewest and truest strokes what his eye had seen aright. Hawthorne's precise meaning may often elude us, but the artist himself is always wide awake, his vision unblurred; and this vision includes a clear comprehension of the ethical meaning which is the soul of artistic work. To his airiest creations he himself stands in the attitude of "the chorus in a classic play, which seems to be set aloof from the possibility of personal concernment." Above all, though the clouds of passion may hide the very skies from his storm-tost sinners and sufferers, the artist's view of moral law and eternal justice is still unobscured. "It is his office to . . . distil in his long brooding thought the whole morality of the performance," says Miles Coverdale.

Among these sketches which we call studies for backgrounds, we are especially interested in the elaborate contribution which Hawthorne originally made to his elder sister's book. It is called "Main Street," and traces, in a panorama, the gradual transformation from the untrodden wilderness to the bustling thoroughfare of to-day. It is an almost equally vivid panorama of the romancer's own growth. Here already the dramatic, the human interest, begins to invade the foreground. His close study of New England history appears. He shows an especial interest in the tragic scenes of persecution and of deluded belief in witchcraft, on which he brooded so long and so fruitfully. Such earlier studies made the "Scarlet Letter" possible at last. Over the brief dialogues between the patient showman and his various critics, Hawthorne's humor plays more broadly than usual. We are reminded here, especially, of the slashing "editorial footnotes" with which he befooled so many serious readers in one of his latest publications, the "Atlantic Monthly" essay, "Chiefly about War Matters." Indeed, Hawthorne's humor usually turns its keenest edge upon his own sober sentiment.

In connection with "Main Street" may perhaps be mentioned the happiest of Hawthorne's purely local pictures, "A Rill from the Town Pump." This was the "monument more lasting than bronze," by which, as he declared, his ungrateful townspeople in Salem would remember him. It has had a curious and manifold fate, having even done service as a temperance tract! It is perhaps the brightest and most agreeable glimpse of Hawthorne as a keen observer and spectator, watching the simple pageant of village life.

Among the most delightful of Hawthorne's short pieces, many are, as it were, dramatized chapters from early New England history. Our readers are no doubt familiar with the

"Maypole of Merry Mount," "The Gentle Boy," "The Gray Champion," with "Lady Eleanore's Mantle," and the other "Province House" legends, "Endicott and the Red Cross," — and we may add "Major Molineux," for which Longfellow expressed his appreciation, greatly to the romancer's delight, in his own "Tales of a Wayside Inn." This lurid night-piece, however, seems in the main a remarkably bold creation of Hawthorne's own fancy. In particular, he has depicted, once for all, those crises in our earlier history most capable of revealing the heroic moral fibre of our forefathers.

Yet his admiration for Endicott's courage, for example, never blinds him to the darker side of Puritanic virtue. Thus, in "Endicott and the Red Cross," the men of Boston are reminded in stirring words how for liberty of conscience they had abandoned home and crossed the seas, but — "Call you this liberty of conscience?" interrupted the Wanton Gospeller, pilloried upon the church steps, at the very crisis of the bold governor's appeal, and "a sad and quiet smile flitted across the mild visage of Roger Williams," who stands for the chorus, for the interested spectator, for the author himself.

We realize the romancer's attachment to the land of his birth, also, from the eternal association of a beautiful truth with the most wonderful natural feature of New Hampshire, in "The Great Stone Face." Incidentally, too, Hawthorne's youthful reverence for Daniel Webster is here recorded. In the "Great Carbuncle," also, a popular legend of the White Hills is crystallized and partly *allegorized;* and here we approach, perhaps, a weaker side of Hawthorne's art.

The predominant influence of Bunyan upon him has been often noted. His debt to the inspired tinker is loyally and most happily paid in "The Celestial Railroad," which seems to bring the beloved apologue down to date, in good faith and earnest. It would have been well if Hawthorne could have rested there. "Little Daffydowndilly," indeed, with the wearily recurring faces of Mr. Toil's brothers, may be harmlessly relegated to a volume for children, though even they would soon learn to skip it! (The juvenile generation educated upon "St. Nicholas" is quick to recognize and decline a thinly sugared sermon. Any doubter is advised to try his beloved "Flowers for Children," or one of Miss Edgeworth's edifying tales, upon his own more enlightened progeny; or, — "Experto crede!") Sometimes, above all in the lovely "Snow Image," the truthful tale stands unspoiled for the childish reader; while the moral, unforced, steals into the very soul of the man who reads over his boy's shoulder. "Feathertop" we accept with a tolerant smile, as a Puritanic transmogrification of Anderson's "Man without Clothes."

But in *e.g.* "Three Wishes," and even in the much-praised "Ethan Brand," we realize that the story is created only for its didactic interpretation at the last. The moral should not be the evident parent of the marvel. Even Hawthorne's voice grows strident, when we thus detect the set purpose to preach. "Pilgrim's Progress" itself, some one has said, is enjoyed chiefly by children, who do not detect its moral purpose, or by "grown-ups," chiefly as a memory of their own childhood.

Distinctly wearisome, despite much wisdom

and power in the details, are the attempts of Hawthorne, starting avowedly with abstractions or unrealities, to give them a visible shape in art. Such are "The Procession of Life," "Earth's Holocaust," "Fancy's Showbox," "The Hollow of Three Hills," and too many others. Of course, even in the least hopeful field, genius may score a success, and of this "A Virtuoso's Collection" is perhaps an example. But certainly one such loose-threaded string of curios was quite enough, and the "Intelligence Office" is a rather feeble repetition on the same theme.

Hawthorne's own strongest interest at this period seems to have been devoted in large part to a certain class of supernatural problems, represented, perhaps, best by "Rapaccini's Daughter," or by "The Artist of the Beautiful." "Dr. Heidegger's Experiment" is a gem in this group (if it may be fairly included), and, besides its brilliant dramatic picture of the four old Ne'er-do-weels and their brief rejuvenation, is important, because Hawthorne in his last years recurred persistently to the same theme, — the elixir of youth. This story has a moral, I believe, but is so well told that we can forget it.

These sketches are the most delicately thought out and wrought out of all his works. They seem to hover upon the very verge and limit of human life and thought and utterance. But they hardly bring back a lesson of vital value to men; and we are constantly tantalized with a hint of allegory unexplained. It is interesting to note that they had this effect even upon their author, when he had had time to forget the precise mood in which they had taken shape. "Upon my honor, I am not quite sure that I entirely comprehend my own meaning in some of these blasted allegories." (Letter of April 13, 1854, quoted in Field's "Yesterdays with Authors.")

As was said before, Hawthorne recurred to these supernatural tendencies in his declining years. But in his central period, in which were produced his four larger masterworks, this mystical — not to say mystifying — vein is in abeyance, and the artist breathes our earthly air, his feet are planted on the bedrock of human nature, his characters and their lives are clearly interpreted to us in the light of our mortal experience. "But that is another story."

As to the vexed question of Hawthorne's morbidness, the answer is already indicated. Despite some very human perversities in the man, as an artist he is sane and healthy. His faith in the eternal goodness and wisdom never fails. Nevertheless, the effect of some of these sketches upon our own youthful imagination was painful and abnormal. A really grewsome image is far more easily summoned up to the childish mind, than explained or allegorized away again. Hawthorne knew Young Goodman Brown saw no evil in the forest, which he did not take thither in his own heart; and almost any man, at forty year, can walk the dimmest wood path, and never wish to glance back and be reassured lest

> "A frightful fiend
> Doth close behind him tread."

But at ten (or twenty) no nervous boy should thread the forest ways in Young Goodman Brown's company. On the closing pages of "The White Old Maid," in the library copy from which I refresh my memories of "Twice-told Tales," a tremulous childish hand has written *An Awful Book*. We feel the shudder of those young nerves. Hawthorne inherited from his Salem lineage, or received as the artist's birthright, a daring imagination, which his healthy, happy, and moral maturity held in firm control. Not all its unearthly visions are fit stimulus for the untrained fancies of our weaker youth. It should be added, however, that these tales were never intended for immature readers, though the pure simplicity of their diction has given some of them a wide currency in the schoolroom. In work expressly intended for childhood Hawthorne is remarkably tender, and scrupulously anxious to exclude what might horrify or perturb an innocent heart.

We would not let any hint of discontent weaken our full utterance of thankfulness to Hawthorne for the many-sided beauty he has created for us. With all the brilliant cleverness of the present generation, devoted above all else to the short story, a volume containing the best twenty, or fifty, American tales would still include a far greater number from this earlier hand than from any other: and no rival has approached the fields he has made peculiarly his own.

Hawthorne's Great Romances

If Hawthorne could revisit us, it would especially tickle his whimsical humor to find his works elevated to the dignity of classics, of which men dare not confess ignorance, and timidly hint disapproval if they feel it. Yet in all such cases the silent dissenters are really numerous. Any man knows among his own kin, his dearest friends, his best pupils perhaps, many whom he can never induce to read his favorite poet, be it Béranger, or Herrick, or Omar Khayyam! Nathaniel Hawthorne seems to me, as to so many others, the most perfect artist in form, the most original creative genius, and the most consummate master of style yet born upon American soil. Yet I doubt if he is really a general favorite, even among refined, thoughtful, and sensitive people.

Perhaps the commonest reason alleged by

those who "cannot read" Hawthorne is his mystical vein. It is only an aggravation, they often say, that the mysticism is after all largely, perhaps wholly, deliberate mystification. Across the clouds of supernaturalism, witchcraft, allegorical symbolism, they too often catch a glimpse of the creative wizard's own face, wreathed in a shrewd incredulous Yankee smile, mocking those who half-accept what he has seemingly tried so hard to make them believe with him.

The first advice we would give to those mature and earnest folk, not wholly devoid of imagination and humor, for whom the Hawthorne hedge has proved impassable, would be, to begin — not with the briefer tales however famous, but — with the great finished romances, and, particularly, with the first and unrivalled masterpiece, the "Scarlet Letter." The man who is unable to finish that should close Hawthorne, if not all romantic literature, in something very like despair, and plunge for a half decade, at least, into the profoundest depths of experience, "Ay, into Life's deep stream."

In that brief and happiest central period of

his life, when three of the four great romances followed each other in such rapid succession, this transcendental vein, be it mystical or mystifying, was almost suppressed. "The artist breathes our earthly air, his feet are planted on the bedrock of human nature, his characters and their lives are clearly interpreted to us in the light of our own mortal experience."

First and greatest of these characters is the heroic woman who, by life-long atonement, makes the shameful scarlet letter an emblem of mercy, love, and self-sacrifice. There is certainly no need — it would be indeed an idle audacity — to offer any detailed explanation of this eternally truthful picture. From the consequences of sin there is no outward escape, no successful flight toward earthly happiness, because the true stigma is burned into the soul itself. For that one mad hour of revived and unbridled hope in the forest, the weaker and guiltier Arthur atones with willing ignominy and death, the stronger woman-nature with many years of self-imposed childless loneliness and ignoble toil.

At the close, as at the beginning, of the tale, Hester stands upon a lonely pedestal of sorrow.

There is no more statuesque woman-shape in all literature. Even there, upon the scaffold, neither the dying Arthur Dimmesdale, nor the wronged husband, old Roger Chillingworth, nor the innocent child Pearl, can distract our sympathy and admiration for an instant from her who dominates them all, and upholds her two loved ones. As I write, the world has hardly done greeting a far more questionable apotheosis of woman triumphant over her own degradation, in "Trilby." But exquisite and appealing as that international romance of Bohemianism is, I am sure Du Maurier himself would have eagerly declared, that in his new field he was still only worthy to be called the gifted pupil of Thackeray, of George Eliot, and of Hawthorne.

A helpful lesson any great work of art undoubtedly has, for the later artist as well as for us who attempt the shaping of nothing save our own characters. The lesson, indeed, is perhaps in its essence the same for both. Let the Notebooks of your experience be as full as possible of accurate observation clearly delineated. For your work of art select and combine, within your finite limitations, that which seems to you above all else eternally true. Call into action natural and helpful impulses, and have no question that the result will be in harmony with everlasting justice and love. Just what form the issue will take, the artist does not always foresee: still less can we forecast our own earthly lot. But in a well-planned romance, as in an earnest life, character works out its own due recompense at last.

It is true that in the "Scarlet Letter," as in "Adam Bede," the chief action of the drama is set in motion by a grievous sin. But sin, evil — and here we touch the heart of Hawthorne's, of George Eliot's, of Emerson's creed — is no malignant, demoniacal power contradicting and thwarting the will of Heaven and accomplishing at last its own purposes. It is but estrangement, distortion, misuse, of impulses not in themselves accurst; and therefore through repentance, atonement, and penance it may work out the blessedness even of the sinner. Hester and Arthur fell through passionate mutual love; and that love, though so sin-stained, is never actually destroyed, but, purified and spiritualized, supports Arthur in death, and Hester in the heavier trial of life. This is not, indeed, a truth which would have been tolerated by the grim Puritans of Endicott's day; but it is undoubtedly what Hawthorne, like George Eliot, Du Maurier, indeed nearly all the true artists and liberal-minded thinkers of our century, believe and teach.

In one outward feature the "Scarlet Letter" is unique among Hawthorne's larger works: perhaps almost unique in the whole history of dramatic fiction. I have quoted already the words in which Miles Coverdale, the gentle poet of the "Blithedale Romance," announces himself as the chorus, witnessing a drama in which he plays no aggressive part. Such a rôle the young photographer holds, amid the more mildly tragic scenes in the "House of the Seven Gables." Beside Miriam and Donatello, both the interested man of marble and the shrinking unwilling Hilda stand as spectators, safely aloof from the current of guilt. But in the "Scarlet Letter" there is no such resting-point for the thought. All in the group of characters are deeply involved; all save the unconscious child Pearl share fully in the guilt.

By his vital interest in the result and his struggle to misdirect it, old Roger Chillingworth loses the power his intellect, and purity in act, should have given him. This makes the "Wind of Destiny" seem more resistless here even than in the other romances, and gives to all the scenes a certain merciless inevitableness which saddens the reader. Yet it is a sadness from which springs full soon an austere and pure satisfaction. Indeed, we are as it were drawn in, ourselves, to hold the balance of justice, or at least to bear witness that Destiny has held it aright.

The "House of the Seven Gables" is, upon the whole, indicative of a happier and less brooding mood of the artist. Phœbe, especially, the cheery little country lass, must have been a delightful surprise even to the romancer, who sometimes repined that he could not move, as an artist, among bright scenes and happy characters. The finale, also, despite the too prolonged death scene, throws at least a mellow autumnal gleam of sunshine even upon the grim doom of heredity which had darkened the earlier pages. The tale is as perfect as the

"Scarlet Letter," the details are more exquisitely wrought; but it has not such an overwhelming power over the reader as the earlier tragedy exerts. Hawthorne felt that it contained more of his truest self.

The "Blithedale Romance" has for its central figure a character, seemingly drawn in part from reality, who wrecks his own and other lives by attempting to be the merciless master of his own fate and theirs. I confess, however, my own observation has not given me many glimpses of such characters as Hollingsworth, and I surely do not yet rightly understand him, since his punishment seems out of all proportion to his acts. Hawthorne is not purely the artist in this book, since there is a large element of realism, drawn from the Brook Farm experience. Even Zenobia could hardly have existed without the traits and tricks contributed to her, as to a second Pandora, by Margaret Fuller. Colonel Higginson has found it easy to catalogue a yet more striking list of differences. We knew Hawthorne was a creative artist, not a reporter. The thrilling closing scene, in which the beautiful Zenobia is found drowned, is also transferred, with hardly a variation in detail, from a real night experience of Hawthorne on Concord River. I am inclined to feel that but for that grim bit of realism in Hawthorne's actual life, — and possibly Margaret Fuller's death by drowning, — the romance might have had a far less tragic close. Zenobia's fate hardly seems inevitable, any more than Hollingsworth's. Altogether, the book is intensely interesting, but not so unquestionably successful, artistically, as any of its three rivals. It seems as if the spirit and the material body of Hawthorne's creation were no longer quite harmonized. Certainly we are less sure of Hawthorne's own happiness in his task while he wrote it, than when Hepzibah, Clifford, and Phœbe were growing to life under his wand.

The "Marble Faun" — known in England as "Transformation" — is the only example of Hawthorne's "third style," as we say in regard to Titian or Murillo; of the period when his eyes were opened to the glories of classical and modern sculpture, to the natural scenery and architecture of Italy. For the background of his last great romance this has undoubtedly provided far greater richness and variety of color and form. (The book has since been utilized — with abundant illustration — as a sort of advanced guide-book for the grand tour of Italy: though Hawthorne's accuracy is hardly of the plodding sort that makes this a safe recourse!) But his art as a romancer had made no corresponding step upward. Indeed, there was doubtless no loftier height left for it to attain. Perhaps the process by which the consciousness of sin educates the soul is more distinctly indicated in the naïve, untutored Donatello, than in the proud, silent, self-contained nature of Hester: but more than indicated it could not be, after all. Not even a Hawthorne could really work out visibly to men's eyes that problem toward whose solution each human soul can but timidly and darkly grope. And even the larger and oft-varied scenery of the "Marble Faun," though so delightful in itself, is perhaps less suited to Hawthorne's small group of perplexed and absorbed human actors, than is the little Puritan settlement on the edge of the mysterious, haunted forest, or the dim, ghost-tenanted old mansion in a quiet Salem street.

As for the plot, we may be wrong, ideally, in demanding anything more than the ethereal or spiritual solution,—the completion of Donatello's education; but there is much truth in the complaint, that all imaginative literature heretofore, all Hawthorne's own stories, and even hints in the course of these scenes themselves, had led us to expect some final explanation as to Donatello's deed and his punishment, which would satisfy — I will not say our curiosity, for we know he is a creature of Hawthorne's, after all, but — our sense of artistic justice and finish. The reluctant final chapter of the second edition, we may all well agree with Hawthorne himself, is worthless. It only shows that in regard to these questions, and as to Miriam's earlier history as well, he had himself nothing to offer us.

The general conclusion, then, appears to be clear. The perfect harmony between the outward materials, the spirit of the drama, and the purpose of the artist, which we feel in the "Scarlet Letter" and the "House of the Seven

Gables," no longer exists intact. It may be that the problems now called up were too great for solution, though this seems hardly consistent, because the flaw so universally felt is rather in the external setting than in the innermost spiritual problem of the book. Hawthorne the man, the scholar, the philosopher, had developed greatly in many directions, — even the writer has many an added grace; but Hawthorne the artist had culminated in Salem and Lenox. Perhaps we may fairly cite in support of this belief, the fact that the rest of Hawthorne's literary life was merely a succession of dissatisfied efforts and uncompleted beginnings. Failing health does not necessarily bring such loss of power, as the beloved exile in Samoa has so happily demonstrated to the last glimmer of the candle.

The Lesser Works

Hawthorne's consummate success, at his best, requires us to mention, at least in passing, his less important utterances. Despite their great interest as materials for the biography, both of man and artist, the Notebooks are hardly more than their title implies. Even the selected English sketches, published in the volume called "Our Old Home," stand almost wholly outside Hawthorne's creative workshop.

The slight outline of New England history, entitled "Grandfather's Chair," could hardly be expected to throw a brilliant light upon the rather obscure and homespun tapestry of our annals. Some scenes and characters, notably Betsy Hull and her dowry of pine-tree shillings, come out in bright relief. The Salem witchcraft and the battle scenes Hawthorne felt to be ill-suited to his audience of children, and he hurries over them as lightly as he can. The half-dozen biographical sketches show, again, that Hawthorne did faithfully and with care whatever he took in hand. But the whole volume leaves us the impression that his romances and tales of fiction are truer than his "True Stories," because more alive.

The "Wonderbook" and "Tanglewood Tales" are more truly Hawthornesque, for despite the classical elements each tale is also a poetic creation. The two modest volumes form together essentially one work, recasting a dozen famous Greek myths, nominally for a group of New England children — really for a much larger circle. It is no more a safe text-book of classical mythology than one which could be made up from Keats' or Tennyson's poems. Rather they are curious examples of the transformation these immortal myths undergo, in the alembic of a modern and Puritanic romancer's mind. We would gladly have, to set beside them, some of the merry recitals of Whittier's "Snowbound" Schoolmaster, wherein

> "Little seemed at best the odds
> 'Twixt Yankee pedlers and old gods:
> . . . And dread Olympus at his will
> Become a huckleberry hill."

These classical stories are, however, a creation of genius, though flung off in a playful hour. Many details from the life with his children in Lenox are utilized, in the interludes of the "Wonderbook" especially, and both his tenderness as a father and his quaint, quiet humor are here seen at their best.

To the four unfinished experiments of Hawthorne's last years, we have already referred.

His own deliberate wish would, no doubt, have been to recall those published, and to destroy them all. They have been discussed quite carefully by the author's son Julian, himself a clever craftsman in literature. They are perhaps most interesting on the technical side, or, indeed, we may almost say, pathologically; especially to those who regard literary creation as a progressive art, which they can acquire and improve upon. It is hardly necessary to add, that this view of the artist's career is very remote from my own. The duty which the younger Hawthorne owes, far more imperatively, to his father's memory, has been already suggested. Some of the deficiencies in the present essay may fairly be charged to its non-performance. There is a sense in which we may claim a right to know so much as can be told concerning the intellectual and artistic biography of our first great imaginative author.

The Artist's Compensations

Both among his shorter stories and in the great romances, Hawthorne's most notable successes are in the tales which have a New England setting. His interest in the life of his bigoted heroic Puritan ancestors was, however, only an artistic sympathy. His reaction from their unbending creed had left him little if any theological convictions. The intervening centuries have already softened somewhat to our view the rugged outlines of their life. A certain glamour of romance begins to fall athwart their homespun costumes, their harsh faces, their unimaginative utterance. At any rate, this New England life — past and present — was the only one the young romancer knew well, and he was aware that the creatures of his imagination, in order to be effectively human, required a certain frame and environment of realism. The history and the landscapes of our Eastern shore he had studied with an accuracy characteristic of the real artist. Nevertheless, the life-drama of Hester, of Hepzibah, of Zenobia, would be essentially the same, whatever the environment. And it is not as a historian, as an antiquarian, nor even as an artist of the picturesque, that Hawthorne attains the lonely heights of genius, but as an observer of the human heart.

H

In a poem, more or less self-revealing in tone, though not confessedly so, Emerson says:

> "Men consort in camp and town,
> But the poet dwells alone."

Yet not one of our New England poets, indeed, no American author save Poe, gives us such an impression of utter solitariness on earth, as does shy, sensitive, wondrously gifted Hawthorne. Emerson himself was the centre of a loyal group whom we call his disciples, though he, like Socrates, would doubtless repudiate the title of Master. If he was himself little dependent upon any living teacher,— though even here Carlyle and the elder Channing might be accounted exceptions,— at least there is a large and congenial company, from Plato to Swedenborg, whose voices blend constantly with Emerson's printed or uttered word, and must have been almost always in his ears.

But even the style of Hawthorne brings us hardly a reminiscence of his reading. Like everything else about him, it has but the delicate aroma of his personality. Nothing precious in it was plainly copied, and very little can be borrowed from it after him by lesser hands. As we linger entranced over his pages, neither he nor we may remember the name or existence of other literary artists. We enter with him directly into the sanctuaries of the soul.

This solitude was his fate on earth. Longfellow was his college associate at Bowdoin. One would think that two such gentle and sensitive natures would surely discover each the other's rare gifts even then. But they confess later, with regret, that they were not drawn closely together in their college days. Many years after, Emerson lived near Hawthorne in the quiet Concord street. They occasionally walked together, but Emerson acquired only a general optimistic faith that the man was "healthier than his books," those books which the tolerant philosopher seems to have pronounced morbid on rather slight — and slighting — perusal!

I think the final judgment will reverse this Emersonian dictum, and say Hawthorne's way of life was a morbid one, or at least would tend to produce morbid men in most cases; but that its hermit-like seclusion and loneliness were destined, in this particular instance, to make possible the most unique and inimitable masterpieces of creative prose that our race has yet to show.

Agassiz compelled a young student of biology to concentrate all his thought, week after week, upon a single fish: and that fish finally taught him the true insight into science. Hawthorne's fate secluded him, year after year, to ponder the structure of the human soul, the problem of sin in the heart. It chanced — if chance there be in the dealings of destiny with us — that the pure spirit and delicately balanced moral nature of Hawthorne carried him triumphantly through this long period of solitary confinement, and enabled him to bring back to the world — not, indeed, a solution for the deepest mystery of Providence, but — artistic studies toward that solution which shall give consolation and pure delight to many a generation after ours.

Not only in youth was Hawthorne, the romancer, a solitary soul. His happy and devoted wife, the children who shared in some degree the literary gift, lived in tenderest harmony with the man. They knew little more than we of the artist who sat silent at his desk, or paced the lonely hill path beneath his pines. It is doubtful whether Hawthorne himself could have rendered any intelligible account, even if he would, of the process through which the materials collected for the great romances acquired a spiritual unity, a soul, as it were, of their own. Herein, to be sure, he is nowise unique. Ask any man who ever shaped a perfect sonnet, a couplet, nay, an apophthegm five words long that drops a true plummet into the depths of life. The mystery is the same in kind, though not in degree.

"These wonders grew as grows the grass."

Exactly. How does the grass grow? Very like the "flower in the crannied wall!" We never hear the answer, but only the echoed question.

As Mr. Stedman makes clear, almost painfully clear, in his sympathetic study of Bayard

Taylor's career, the artist must often choose — or destiny chooses for him — between the fullest development and all-sided enjoyment of life among men, and the complete consecration of himself to that unique flower of genius which is implanted in his own soul. The latter choice is perhaps more apt to assure long-lasting fame. The single, narrower devotion to creative efforts builds (to change the metaphor) the loftier and more enduring monument.

Lowell, with natural gifts almost or quite as unique, made, on the whole, the other choice. He never found even such half seclusion as he ridiculed in Thoreau. Consequently, Hosea Biglow's dialect poetry, the sympathetic studies of great poets, the slashing critical reviews, the editor's, the professor's, the diplomatist's work, his frank letters, even the great memorial addresses and odes, are comparatively perishable assurances of Lowell's equipment for the one great task which he never essayed: whether epic, drama, or romance we shall not know. Too late, with divided energies and world-wide interests, he attempted, *e.g.* in the "Cathedral," to reconsecrate himself to that highest art which demands single-hearted service. But few men, surely, will recall the first reading of this or any other poem of Lowell as an epoch in their lives. We may fancy we have outgrown "Hiawatha" or "Evangeline," "Elaine" or even "In Memoriam." But imagine any one of these utterly blotted out of Past as well as Present! Would it not leave as real a gap as the death of an old friend?

Whittier, even, with no such rare genius as either Hawthorne or Lowell, after a lifetime of distraction and unpoetic strife, has, after all, set one tenderly truthful picture — "Snow-bound" — in that little circle of ever-familiar scenes which are, as it were, the windows of our imagination. No one work of Lowell's, it seems to me, has gained, or can ever gain, quite this position in the average New Englander's or American's memory. But, surely, the tragic group upon the scaffold at the close of the "Scarlet Letter," at least, has a place of honor among our indelible and universal remembrances.

We do not say Lowell either should have made, or could have made, in youth the same choice as Hawthorne. Indeed, Hawthorne repined bitterly at what he called his own "cursed habits of solitude." But, at least, there is a Compensation, as Emerson uses the word, more complete, indeed, than the recluse in his loneliest hours is wont clearly to foresee. We may sometimes reverse the emphasis in Goethe's famous couplet:

> "A talent is in solitude developed,
> But in the stream of life a character,"

and read:

> "In life's full stream a character develops;
> — Only in solitude doth genius bloom."

IV

LONGFELLOW

Longfellow's Youth

The bust of Longfellow, set up in the Poets' Corner of Westminster Abbey, was, I believe, the first memorial of any other than an Englishman ever admitted to that doubly sacred precinct. Perhaps the general feeling of approval at this act is itself among the singer's greatest triumphs. He, first of all Americans, has produced works equally and perfectly familiar in both lands, through both hemispheres. There lived in England, in his time, at least one greater literary artist, as Longfellow himself loyally declared in his sonnet "Wapentake": the Touching of the Shield. That challenge to Tennyson is, as he explains, no defiance, but

> "In sign
> Of homage to the mastery which is thine
> In English song."

Others, like — let us say — Browning, have essayed more successfully, as Whittier expresses it,

> "To drop a plummet line below
>   Our common world of joy and woe,
> A more intense delight or deeper grief to find"

— if that be the true proof of greatness. But Longfellow has uttered the sincerest and purest feelings of the uncounted millions, all around the globe, that use our English speech. Some, ay many, of his best-beloved lyrics seem destined to live, for wider helpfulness in the teeming future,

> "As long as the heart has passions,
>   As long as life has woes."

This, alone, would be a blessed earthly lot for any man. But it is not all. The life of Longfellow was, itself, a noble work of art: perhaps as encouraging and inspiring as any our young civilization has yet to show. From that life, and from his poetic work as well, there are precious lessons to be drawn, not merely for the humble heart everywhere,

> "That hopes, and endures, and is patient,"

but for the aspiring soul, for the ambitious artist, for the wise and strong among mankind. It is above all a story of untiring preparation and triumphant fulfilment of a sacred mission. We need not fear to call attention, once again, to the moral, the ethical tone, which all our Puritan poets strike in harmony. And the especial lesson of Longfellow's beautiful life is perhaps that expressed in one of the poems often called, half-jestingly, his "psalms" (though, indeed, he himself freely uses that title for them in his diary):

> "We have not wings, we cannot soar;
> But we have feet to scale and climb
> By slow degrees, by more and more,
> The cloudy summits of our time.
>
> "The heights by great men gained and kept
> Were not attained by sudden flight,
> But they, while their companions slept,
> Were toiling upward in the night."

Not that any lifelong exertion would have produced among us other Longfellows. Let us be thankful for each great creative artist as a distinct miracle wrought for us all. But the divine spark entrusted to him was fed to a clear, ever-brightening flame by unbroken years of generous devotion, of arduous study, of unremitting effort. Such consecration to our highest possibilities is in itself the truest success.

> "No endeavor is in vain:
> The reward is in the doing,
> And the rapture of pursuing
> Is the prize the vanquished gain!"

The great triumphs of Longfellow's maturity are familiar to all. All our hearts have throbbed to the music of his "Psalm of Life." To every man's youth the cry of Excelsior has echoed far up the heights, even if the voice no longer falls on our memory like a falling star. It is especially, therefore, to the scholarly side of Longfellow's life, and to his thorough preparation, that I would call attention here.

How much we all owe to a pious, thoughtful ancestry can never be fully determined. Even among the half-dozen kindred spirits popularly grouped as the New England poets, the youthful Longfellow seems remarkable for natural gentleness and innocence, for an instinctive choice of things pure and noble, for innate refinement and scholarly tastes.

His seventeenth-century ancestors dwelt, like the Whittiers, and also the Lowells, in the Merrimac valley, at Newbury. His great-grandfather, Stephen Longfellow, a Harvard graduate, was called to Portland, as a teacher, in 1744. A second Stephen was state senator, judge, etc., and a third, the poet's father, was again a Harvard graduate, an active lawyer, a congressman while Henry was studying at Bowdoin, later president of the Maine Historical Society, and a universally respected citizen of 'Portland. Longfellow's earliest associations were evidently more favorable to literary culture than those of Whittier, or even of Hawthorne.

Of his native city, Portland, we have loving glimpses, especially in "My Lost Youth," where he sighs:

> "Often I think of the beautiful town
> That is seated by the sea";

but there is nowhere a trace of the irritation and disappointed pride that mingle with Hawthorne's half-tender, half-satirical memories of Salem.

It may be due to his birth in sight of the Atlantic waves, that Longfellow — though otherwise not a close student of outward nature, one, indeed, who was more at home even from boyhood in a library than in the woods and fields — yet constantly recurs wistfully to the "Secret of the Sea." The poems which bring the first unmistakable announcement that a vigorous creative artist has come, are the "Skeleton in Armor" and "The Wreck of the Hesperus," both distinctively sea poems. Indeed, if we were to cull with care from the goodly Corpus of his verse all those poetical figures which he had drawn, not from the suggestions of earlier authors, but from his own observation in the open air, we should surely find that a very large proportion of them had to do with the

> "Beauty and mystery of the ships,
> And the magic of the sea."

Thus in "Miles Standish" the most vivid and fitting image is in the march of the angry little captain and his troop up the coast, in the gray of the dawn, while

> "Under them loud on the sands the serried billows advancing,
> Fired along the line, and in regular order retreated."

We may be sure these verses were composed to the thunderous accompaniment of the Atlantic billows themselves, upon the beloved shore of Nahant.

Longfellow was only fourteen when he entered Bowdoin College, in the same class with his elder brother Stephen. The latter, by the way, was much nearer to Hawthorne in those years, though the two men of genius were upon friendly terms. The letters to his parents during his college life were amusingly sedate, bookish, — one is tempted to add, — priggish! There is one curious reminder, how different was the undergraduate of seventy years ago from the modern athletic type. "The government, seeing that something must be done to induce the students to exercise, recommended a game of ball now and then." And the context leaves the impression, that the result was an unwelcome draught upon the young scholar's literary leisure!

Even before he entered college, some verses of the boy rhymer had appeared in the Portland papers. During his four years at Bowdoin he acquired a real, though somewhat slender, literary reputation. Seventeen of his poems appeared in the "United States Literary Gazette" (Boston) alone. These undoubtedly showed more refinement and taste than ordinary undergraduate verses; but they give little promise of originality and force,— unless, as a kindly editor wrote him at that time, "An exuberance of blossoms is a good promise for fruit." Bryant's influence is especially evident. In general, any work of this period would hardly have been preserved but for the writer's later fame. Only seven of the early poems, "all written before the age of nineteen," were included by Longfellow in his collected works. The "Burial of the Minnisink" (an Indian chief) is perhaps most interesting, especially as a prophecy of the poet's greatest popular success, "Hiawatha."

But it is far more significant, that, for nearly a dozen following years (1826 – 1837), Longfellow wrote no original poetry at all: he had discovered that he had as yet no message to men: no adequate knowledge of life. So Schiller said later of his youthful drama, "The Robbers": "I attempted to draw men before I had known any." Longfellow was more timely wise. He produced no more immature verse. Instead, he was devoting himself to an exhaustive study of modern languages and literatures, which soon left him without a rival in America, save Ticknor, in his chosen field.

In this happy turn of his life, fortune, or Providence, had a manifest share. Upon his graduation, his father hoped he would study law. So it was with Holmes, and with Lowell. His own heart was set on a post-graduate course in literature at Harvard. But Bowdoin had just decided to create a professorship of modern languages, and this was informally offered to the precocious youth, who at eighteen years of age had just graduated fourth in a class of thirty-eight. He was required first to spend a series of years in preparing himself abroad.

So in April, 1826, he left home, to remain

over three years in France, Spain, Italy, and Germany. He lived comfortably, often in refined native families in each country. His letters of introduction made him known to the best American society in Europe, *e.g.* the Irvings and Everetts in Spain. But he devoted himself indefatigably to the mastery of languages and literatures. There can hardly be a severer test for youthful character than such a lonely student-life in foreign lands. Longfellow could have echoed young Milton's boastful citation from Horace, "*Cœlum non animum muto dum trans mare curro.*"

The next six years, 1829–1835, Longfellow held the professorship at Bowdoin. In 1831 he was happily wedded. His married home was a delightful old Brunswick house, shaded by gigantic elms. At least the ample mansion seemed venerable, and the elms were enormous in 1892, in which year the present writer was a Bowdoin professor, and, as it chanced, beheld one of these noble trees toppled over in a cyclone, and crushing in the roof of the historic abode!

The bibliography of his work published during this period will surprise those who know him only as a popular poet. It shows that, besides faithful service in the teacher's chair, he was completing his systematic study of the chief languages and literatures of Europe. For practical instruction he wrote an Italian grammar in French, adapted an elementary French grammar, and edited French, Spanish, and Italian books for reading.

He printed six important essays in the old "North American Review" — that solid repository of general scholarship which we sadly miss. Longfellow's papers on the origin and history of the French, Italian, and Spanish languages are partly philological, though illuminated by literary taste. "Old English Romances" and a later paper on Anglo-Saxon literature (1838) show that his own direct poetic ancestry was not omitted from the cycle of his studies. "Spanish Devotional and Moral Poetry" gives more scope to his masterly skill in metrical translation. Especially, a number of sonnets are here exquisitely rendered.

It seems important to call due attention to this long and laborious apprenticeship, served by our most popular poet. Simplicity is of two kinds, and is attained by two very different paths. Will Carleton's "Betsey and I are out" and "The Birds of Killingworth" are equally easy reading. Both appeal effectively to the elemental instincts of humanity. One has the crude and homely simplicity of natural feeling, the other the crystalline perfection, in form and expression, that marks consummate art. That is a perfectly healthful and natural interest which the first glance at a Rogers statuette arouses, and usually satisfies. But we can draw a much higher enjoyment from the Hermes of Praxiteles and the Melian Aphrodite. My present point is, that between "The Burial of the Minnisink" and "The Skeleton in Armor" lay a dozen years of just such study of form in the works of the earlier masters as a precocious young composer gains by steadfast devotion to Mozart and Beethoven, or a clever natural artist by "drawing from the antique."

Especial interest attaches to the essay, "Defence of Poetry," published in the "North American," January, 1832. Beginning in traditional reviewers' fashion with a notice of Sir Philip

Sidney's "Defence of Poesy" (then just reprinted), this is really the frankly uttered Credo of a patriotic, ambitious young American, upon the threshold of our Golden Age of letters — in which he is himself to be the central figure. •It should be studied side by side with Emerson's oration, "The American Scholar," which was not delivered until 1837. Yet the real sunrise of our national literature had come, ten years before Longfellow wrote this paper, with the appearance, almost simultaneously, of Cooper's "Spy," Irving's "Sketch Book," and Bryant's first volume of poems, including "The Ages," "To a Waterfowl," and "Thanatopsis."

Mr. Longfellow's resolute abstention in later years from anything like literary criticism justifies me in calling more carefully to others' attention this early and little-read study. As has happened constantly in all ages, the poet-philosopher finds his generation an all too sordid and practical folk. "We are swallowed up," he says, "in schemes for gain, and engrossed with contrivances for bodily enjoyment." So we are, still! We have ourselves echoed this familiar cry. "The true glory of a nation is moral and intellectual preëminence," he cries, with all the zeal of fresh discovery. That sentence may have suggested the title for the great Fourth of July speech against war, called "The True Grandeur of Nations," delivered thirteen years later by Longfellow's beloved friend, Charles Sumner. The practical utility of the fine arts is insisted on, in words that glow with color. "Does not the pen of the historian perpetuate the fame of the hero and the statesman? Do not their names live in the song of the bard?... Does not the spirit of the patriot and the sage, looking from the painted canvas or eloquent from the marble lip, fill our hearts with veneration for all that is great in intellect and godlike in virtue?" Truly this is no shrill cry of "Art for Art's Sake," whatever that shibboleth may mean. At any rate, with Longfellow we are still safe in the happy days "when Art was still Religion!"

The creative Artist, he insists, must be true to nature, though he cannot be merely true to fact, — a profoundly important distinction. No woman, as he indicates, was ever so perfect as to be the sole model for the Venus de' Medici. So his Evangeline is "false to fact," if you like. She never existed, nor did Elaine! But both are loftily true to ideal womanhood.

Poetry, Longfellow reminds us, is older than our earliest traditions. He believes, apparently, in a peaceful pastoral Age of Gold, before the wars began that furnished materials for Iliads and Nibelungenlieds. In those happy days Imagination awoke in man, shaping the nymph for the gushing fountain, giving a personal life to grove and sea billow, creating a goddess, to thank her for the bounteous harvests as *her* creation. So poesy began.

And poetry is thus the eternal mirror of man's inner feelings and outward life. Hence it is also the most authentic material for history, since "historic facts are chiefly valuable as exhibiting intellectual phenomena." Indeed, a great poem, like the "Iliad," the "Nibelungen," the "Poema del Cid," or the songs of the Troubadours, may often be essentially our only memorial from a phase of human life and thought which has forever passed away. Poetry and pottery are the two records of man's existence which are essentially indestructible. From the dust of Hissarlik we have gathered shards of the lacrimatory urn which received Andromache's tears for Hector: at least, no one can ever disprove our fond belief; but in the "Iliad" the tears themselves flow ever afresh, and ours with them.

Poetry, he continues, should be truly national. Thus the so-called "pastoral" verse is mostly affectation in our climate. Walpole's witty remark is quoted with approval. "Our poets learnt their trade of the Romans, and so adopted the terms of their masters. They talk of shady groves, purling streams, and cooling breezes, — and we get sore throats and agues in attempting to realize these visions."

"We wish our native poets would give a more national character to their writings. This is peculiarly true in descriptions of natural scenery. . . . Let us have no more skylarks and nightingales." Longfellow is here writing the epitaph for his own boyish verses with the rest. Indeed, "the precocity of our writers" is deplored with unmistakable emphasis in this paper. In his "Angler's Song,"

> "Upward speeds the morning lark
> To its silver cloud,"

(1826), and the mock-nightingale's falsetto also could very likely be discovered, by careful search, among these youthful strains. Nor did he fully take to heart his own warning, even now. Long after, when the Prelude to "Voices of the Night" had appeared, Margaret Fuller reminded him sharply that New Englanders kept no record of Pentecost, and neither knew nor cared whether

> "Bishops' caps have golden rings."

The more important lesson with which Longfellow returned later to verse was that humanity, not unconscious nature, is the centre of all rational interest. To quote again from the Prelude, the poet has heard the admonition of far-off voices, — perhaps the voices of the "dead poets, who are still living," whom he later apostrophizes in a noble sonnet:

> "Learn, that henceforth thy song shall be,
> Not mountains capped with snow,
> Nor forests sounding like the sea,
> Nor rivers flowing ceaselessly. . . .
>
> "Look, then, into thine heart, and write!
> Yes, into life's deep stream!"

The essay we are discussing faces in the same direction. Though poetry is still praised as the fit companion for weary men's hours of idleness and of dreamy ease, its true office is a higher one — even the highest. . . . "There is something immortal in us, something which amid the din of life urges us to aspire after the attributes of a more spiritual nature. Let the cares and business of the world sometimes sleep, for this sleep is the awakening of the soul."

Longfellow's moral earnestness even leads him in this paper to what is rare indeed from his pen: the severest criticism of another poet. "No writer has done half so much," he says, "to corrupt the literary taste, as well as the moral principles of our country, as the author of 'Childe Harold.'" In Wordsworth he finds a healthful antidote, but urges that the young writer "should leave the present age and go back to the olden time. He should make, not the writings of an individual, but the whole body of English classical literature, his study."

It is generally felt that such warnings concerning Byron are no longer needed. He is gone quite out of fashion. Indeed, it is rather a pity that "Childe Harold," at least, is not studied more than it is. One quality in it, especially, a large stateliness of style, a free swift movement that finds the great Spenserean stanza not too ample, is almost unrivalled still. How many poets have ever attained such majesty as Byron in the familiar lines,

"There is a pleasure in the pathless wood," . . .

or many another such strophe? And as for the tendency to meditation — after Wordsworth's fashion — over inanimate nature, Bryant, Emerson, Longfellow himself, and their disciples have brought quite enough of this to New England.

Altogether, despite one or two bits of rhetorical and evidently rather delectable pessimism over "these practical days," wherein the divine stream of poesy has "spread itself into stagnant pools," the paper should have aroused bright anticipations of the approaching time, when this scholar-philosopher was himself to return to the task of creating poetry.

In the year 1835, which closed his Brunswick experience, Longfellow published "Outre-Mer," a rather sentimental, loosely strung series of sketches from a traveller's notebook. The best of it suggests a comparison with Irving's "Sketch Book," which Longfellow has told us was the first work to influence him vitally, and which had appeared when the poet was an undergraduate at Bowdoin. "Outre-Mer" is in great part

> "Full of a young man's joy to be
> Abroad in the world, alone and free."

It has several bright pictures of the "lands beyond the sea." Normandy seen from the top of a diligence was almost a *terra incognita* then, the cemetery of Père-la-Chaise, also, not too hackneyed a subject. (Florence and Rome, even then, were passed over as an all-too-familiar "traveller's tale.") But the little volume was largely pieced out — not to say padded — with chapters upon Devotional

Poetry of Spain, Ancient Spanish Ballads, the Trouvères, etc., giving a strong flavor of bookishness to the whole. Longfellow is indeed, above all else, a bookman: he usually sees art and nature best through other poets' rhymes, as he himself says in old age:

> "I turn the world round with my hands,
> Reading these poets' rhymes . . .
> And see when looking with their eyes,
> Better than with my own!"

Another period of travel and study, in preparation for the Harvard professorship, now intervened. These two years (April, 1835 – October, 1836) were darkened by the death of Longfellow's young wife, which occurred in Holland, November, 1835. There is a brief allusion to her in "Footsteps of Angels," as

> "The Being Beauteous,
> Who unto my youth was given,
> More than all things else to love me,
> And is now a saint in Heaven."

The next seven years, 1836–1843, until Longfellow's second marriage, constitute the next period of his life, including his return to poetry.

The verses called "Flowers" were actually the first written, being sent with some autumn blossoms to a friend in October, 1837. He had established himself the previous summer as a lodger in Craigie House, later to be his own, and so long associated inseparably with his life and his work. The full reäwakening of his poet-nature came, however, a year later in the "Psalm of Life." The first poem is as finished as a Dutch miniature, showing unlimited pains in polishing, — and perhaps diligent use of a rhyming dictionary! But it is as cold, as lifeless, and almost as scentless as a wreath of artificial blossoms.

The "Psalm of Life" is far less polished and fluent. Rather it suggests a tumultuous eagerness for expression. We, of course, can never read it as it was first read then, much less realize fully the spirit in which it was written. But the very crudeness of parts reveals the throb and heat behind it.

And its lesson was more needed then. The "mournful numbers" against which it protests filled the air about him with their sickly sentimentality. To us "life *is* real, life *is* earnest," and the literary life, at least, in America is infinitely more real and earnest, because Longfellow sang for almost half a century after those days. This very poem is in part another protest against the influence of Byron, which was then still supreme. Spiritually, the poem justifies the prompt and loud acclaim with which it was hailed. As to its form, we should wish (did not old association make it sacred just as it is) that Longfellow had thus early hit upon the measure, very near to this trochaic form outwardly, far above it in natural fitness and force: the measure in which many of his deepest personal feelings afterward took shape without effort. How near it lay! The very words of the Psalm struggle against the trochaic lockstep:

> "Fór the soul is dead that slumbers,
>   Aṅd things are not what they seem." . . .

> "Iṅ the world's broad field of battle,
>   Iṅ the bivouac of life."

And how triumphantly afterward, in "The Bridge" or "The Day is Done," the verses escaped the fetters of an un-English rhythm:

> "As sweeping and eddying through them,
>   Rose the belated tide,
> And streaming into the moonlight
>   The seaweed floated wide."

If we have set our quotation so that the poet's thoughts are likened to drifted seaweed, it is only what he has done with full elaboration elsewhere! "To the River Charles" shows what could be made of the trochees with more technical skill and less eager rush of thought: but artificial they must always be, since they strive against the tide of our native speech.

From this time the story is a brightening one for many a year. The romance "Hyperion," published in 1839, is a reminiscence especially of that last lonely year in Europe. But a future of hope softens its sadness. In Mary Ashburton is a delineation of Frances Appleton, whom the poet had met in 1837, in Switzerland, as a girl of nineteen, and whom he was to marry in 1843. Still, the incidents of "Hyperion," we must believe, are altogether fictitious. The book is the most important among Longfellow's prose works. "Kavanagh," written ten years later, is a rather slight and pallid novelette, generously characterized by Emerson as "the best sketch we have seen in the direction of the American novel." Both tales demonstrate negatively and finally (though agreeably) that Longfellow's chief energies were rightly devoted to verse.

"Voices of the Night" appeared later, in 1839. In them there is still a cloying sweetness, a love of graceful form and melodious sound for their own sake, sufficient to recall the precocious versifier of undergraduate days. The very title is daintily chosen, and has dragged the closing verses of the Prelude away from its chief purport, namely, that Life is the sole worthy theme of the poet.

"The Skeleton in Armor" and "The Wreck of the Hesperus" presently bring the full assurance that the graceful translator, and even the learned and persuasive Humanist, will be forgotten, since the poet's heart has found voice. The rest of Longfellow's literary life seems to follow as naturally as the unfolding, leaf by leaf, of the *Victoria regia!* Here Longfellow's youth, his apprentice years, may be said to end: and how full those years were

K

of toil, self-repression, and wise silences, is not even yet generally recognized in adequate degree.

Longfellow's Maturity

The entire life of Longfellow was directed, with remarkable consistency and singleness of purpose, to literary studies, out of which his own creative and imaginative work seemed to grow as naturally as the fruit ripens upon a firm-rooted tree. His perusal of literature was not critical, in any severely analytical and destructive sense, much less so than in Lowell's case. What he disapproved, he quietly avoided; at whatever springs he found vigor and encouragement, he drank deep. Hence came, in part, his remarkable success as a translator.

Though happy in love and friendship, and enjoying an ever-widening popularity, Mr. Longfellow shrank from anything like a public appearance. Even in the all-absorbing agitation against human slavery, this lifelong friend of Charles Sumner took part only in a single, almost accidental, series of poems, written on a lonely sea-voyage. To be sure, these ranged him unmistakably on humanity's side, and he was doubtless "fanatic named and fool" therefor, to quote a phrase Lowell uses of Wendell Phillips. Not very long afterward, however, the Abolitionists themselves were denouncing the gentle poet, when he yielded to his publishers' desire, and omitted the "Poems on Slavery" from the collected edition of his works. Of his brother-poet Whittier's confessed taste for politics, he had not the slightest share. Indeed, Whittier's proposal that he should stand as candidate for Congress was rejected with something very like terror.

The poet's second marriage, in 1843, appears to have been an ideal one in every respect. Craigie House and the lands about it came to Longfellow as his wife's dower. Of the bridal journey we have a memorial in the poem, "The Arsenal at Springfield." It was the bride who noted the likeness of the shining musket-barrels on the walls to organ pipes, imagined how grim a melody Death would play upon them, and besought her poet to sing the glories of peace. For every such glimpse as this into the inner workshop of the artist we proffer our deepest thanks. That we owe more than this, a hundred-fold, to the poet's wife, we may be sure. Truly

> "Each man's chimney is his Golden Milestone;
> Is the central point from which he measures
> Every distance
> Through the gateways of the world around him."

And the happy glow of Longfellow's hearth-fire in Craigie House has helped him to make all the ways of this world brighter and plainer for humanity. There are, however, but few direct memorials of his own home-happiness among Longfellow's published poems. The "Children's Hour" is doubtless the best known. In one of his rare odes, called "To a Child," are bright glimpses of the home, and allusions to the earlier time when it had been Washington's headquarters. The child (1845) must have been the poet's eldest son Charles.

Longfellow told William Winter that he wrote some verses for himself alone, too personal and intimate for publication. This is an interesting assurance that the poetic utterance becomes, for the true poet, the natural and final expression of his inmost feelings. This was true especially, in his case, of a form peculiarly artificial, never likely to be widely popular, — the sonnet.

Longfellow was the greatest master of this delicate structure who has appeared in America. Indeed, he seems to me one of the most perfect artists, as to form and finish, within the sonnet's "narrow plot of ground" in all the history of English letters. There is a fascination about this form of verse which cannot be described to those who have never felt it. I firmly believe there is an occult, but profound, relation between the close-woven octette and sextette on the one hand, and the natural scope and measure of an adequate poetic thought on the other: a relation not fathomed, if dreamed of, in our philosophy. The rise of the thought, the transition, yet without a break, at the ninth line is, perhaps, the final test as to the fitness of the idea for this mould. Longfellow seems to have found the sonnet a necessity to him, to enshrine, and so banish, a thought which haunted him: nor is he at all alone in this feeling.

Thus, at the half-way house of life, he composed verses not meant for the world's eye, containing a confession of ambition baffled as yet. This sonnet was written in 1842, during a six months' stay at the Rhineland water cure of Marienberg. The title is a reminiscence of the first line in the "Divine Comedy."

Mezzo Cammin

"Half of my life is gone, and I have let
    The years slip from me and have not fulfilled
    The aspirations of my youth, to build
Some tower of song with lofty parapet.
Not indolence, nor pleasure, nor the fret
    Of restless passions that would not be stilled,
    But sorrow, and a care that almost killed,
Kept me from what I may accomplish yet.
    Though, half way up the hill, I see the Past
Lying beneath me with its sounds and sights;
    A city in the twilight dim and vast,
With smoking roofs, soft bells, and gleaming lights,
    And hear above me on the autumnal blast
The cataract of Death far thundering from the heights."

There is no more natural utterance in all his verse than the poem beginning,

"I said unto myself, 'If I were dead
    What would befall these children?'"

But a still surer example of his recourse to the sonnet, purely as a release from haunting thoughts, is the utterance of his undying grief for the beautiful woman who had made his home so bright through eighteen years, and who was then eighteen years dead. This again was meant only for his own eye: and was found in his portfolio after his departure, though written in 1879

> "In the long, sleepless watches of the night
> A gentle face — the face of one long dead —
> Looks at me from the wall."

In this sonnet only ("The Cross of Snow") does he allude to the terrible death of his wife:

> "Soul more white
> Never through martyrdom of fire was led
> To its repose."

The allusion in "Footsteps of Angels" to the wife of his early youth was also written long after her death. The only poem which can be considered an utterance of living love is the sonnet "The Evening Star."

In this same year of 1879 there is an entry in Longfellow's diary, showing how little of the mystic there was in the man who once calls Emerson's lectures "all dreamery after all." "I was eighteen years old when I took my college degree; eighteen years afterward I was married for the second time; I lived with my wife eighteen years, and it is eighteen years since she died. . . . And then . . . I was eighteen years professor in the college here, and have published eighteen separate volumes of poems. This is curious; the necromancers would make a good deal out of it: I cannot make anything at all."

The tragic and awfully sudden loss of his wife, in July 1861, made a gulf in Longfellow's life which was never filled. Yet a thoughtful comparison of *e.g.* the "Wayside Inn" with his earlier work will show, I think, that the man's suffering was the world's gain. His nature was so pure, so manly, so heroic, that the call to suffer and be strong only aroused the chords and harmonies of ever deeper sympathy with all who must learn the same bitter lesson.

Nor is it generally felt in this case, — as is often said of Lowell, and sometimes of Whittier, — that the avocations of the man hampered or dwarfed the full development and fruitfulness of the poet. Rather, his work as a teacher stimulated his studies, and those studies reached the sources from which much of his best material was drawn. To be sure, after the great triumph won with " Evangeline," in 1847, and the approaching completion of " Hiawatha," in 1855, he felt justified in devoting the rest of life wholly to creative work; and in the latter year was succeeded in his college chair by the beloved brother-poet Lowell. But the " Saga of King Olaf," *e.g.* we owe to the Scandinavian scholar as clearly as to the Puritan singer. Indeed, of all the

> " Tales those merry guests
> Told to each other "

in the Wayside Inn, only one, the " Birds of Killingworth," was absolutely original. How far Longfellow was from regretting or apologizing for such dependence, we see from his allusion to Shakspeare's similar relation to the " Decameron " and its rivals:

> " Nor were it grateful to forget
> That from these reservoirs and tanks
> Even imperial Shakspeare drew
> His Moor of Venice and the Jew,

> And Romeo and Juliet,
> And many a famous comedy."

This is said in the interlude of sharp discussion that follows the delightful transfusion (or indeed transfiguration) of Ser Federigo and his falcon.

And yet Longfellow was indeed a creative artist, whose soul was greater than, was truly master of, all the materials it drew from world-wide wanderings. Any one who doubts it should turn to such a page as that which holds the last tribute to Hawthorne. Here is no single glance away from the village of Concord, save one at the most familiar of all our nursery tales, "The unfinished window in Aladdin's tower." Yet the artist and the man is nowhere more fully present. Nowhere in literature do I find a better metaphor from outward nature than in the brief line:

> "The hill-top hearsed with pines."

It is true, however, that Longfellow, though a master-artist, was not a great original thinker. But while this is to be largely conceded, it has often been greatly overstated. Even if Longfellow had been a mere translator, our debt to him would still be great. There are many warm lovers of Uhland, who take even more delight in the "Luck of Edenhall" than in "Das Glück von Edenhall." In some minor lyrics it is certainly true that Longfellow's versions more than replace their originals. As an interpreter of foreign literatures and races he has broadened our national culture and habits of thought more, perhaps, than any other one man. His great version of Dante is but a partial success, for it assays the unattainable. The poetic charm of the great mediæval singer is lost, but at least his every thought is rendered intelligible; and Dante was the master-mind, as well as the master-poet, of his age. But the "Saga of King Olaf," or the miracle-play in the "Golden Legend," could only have been created by a true scholar, who had taken up into himself the spirit of a whole literature, of a whole epoch, and who was also a creative artist, able to give that spirit a freshly fashioned and beautiful form. In "Hiawatha," indeed, all the Indian lore of Schoolcraft and the rest was but mere unwrought clay for the potter. Here, almost everything is due to him who first gave it poetic beauty and spiritual meaning.

And, though we omit from view every poem, great and little, which even seems to gain a suggestion from an alien source, there still remains a Longfellow, dear to all our hearts, who interprets to us, in words grown as familiar as the prayer of childhood, merely the truest voices of our own souls. Such utterances are "The Children's Hour," "Weariness," "Golden Milestone," "Resignation," "The Bridge," "The Rainy Day," and a hundred more. For every New Englander, at least, Longfellow's poetry is literally what Shelley said of Keats':

> "He is made one with nature. There is heard
> His voice in all her music."

The diary of Longfellow has already been repeatedly quoted. It is usually very brief and meagre in form. He once intimates that the fear of future publicity restrains him from entering in it any hint of his inner life: and even of his external existence it is a very incomplete chronicle, as he there remarks. This journal was excellently edited by the poet's brother Samuel, who also supplemented it helpfully from the letters placed at his disposal. But we learn little, disappointingly little, on the whole, in regard to the poet's artistic processes.

I remember his telling me, in the only personal talk I ever had with him, that he filed and polished a poem, soon after it was first composed, until he had perfected it to the extent of his powers; but rarely touched it again: certainly not after publishing it. He said he realized that the readers of a poem acquired a right to the poet's work in the form they had learned to love. Moreover, he had felt that Bryant and Whittier hardly seemed happy in these belated revisions. He mentioned especially Bryant's "Waterfowl,"

"As darkly limned upon the ethereal sky." . . .

He himself preferred the original reading "painted on." It must be conceded that there are weighty examples, like Tennyson, upon the opposite side. Still, it is oftener true, that the artist himself becomes another man, and should let the work of his earlier self stand, faulty though it must seem to him. Schiller felt this, and expressed it strongly, in regard to his "Don Carlos."

It is a general and no doubt correct impression, that most of Longfellow's lyrical work was done with ease, and required little revision.

> "As come the white sails of ships,
>   O'er the ocean's verge;
> As comes the smile to the lips,
>   The foam to the surge, —
> So come to the poet his songs." . . .

To this there are, of course, exceptions; but *e.g.* the "Arrow and the Song" darted into his mind as instantaneously as the shaft itself pierces the heart of an oak. Another illustration is especially instructive: the more as it marks an important stage in his progress.

In the journal, under December 17, 1839, we read of the shipwrecks reported in the papers, and of bodies washed ashore, "one lashed to a piece of the wreck. There is a reef called Norman's Woe" (where many wrecks occurred) . . . "among others the schooner 'Hesperus.' . . . I must write a ballad on this; also two others, — 'The Skeleton in Armor' and 'Sir

Humphrey Gilbert.'" We see that the news of the day has drawn the poet's thoughts to the mysterious terrors of the deep. The most vivid and painful subject of the three lies crystallizing in the author's mind for a fortnight. Then (December 30), "Last evening . . . I sat till twelve o'clock by my fire, smoking, when suddenly it came into my mind to write the 'Ballad of the Schooner Hesperus,' which I accordingly did. Then I went to bed, but could not sleep. New thoughts were running in my mind, and I got up to add them to the ballad. It was three by the clock. I then went to bed and fell asleep. I feel pleased with the ballad. It hardly cost me an effort. It did not come into my mind by lines, but by stanzas." January 2d (three days later), a fair copy is made, doubtless with some filing and polishing also of the details. The evening of the 4th Hawthorne, then in the Boston custom house, dropping in, hears it with delight, and says he will give it to the skipper of every craft he boards in Boston harbor. (Yet it must be said the poem was hardly one to cheer the sea-bound mariners upon our bleak coast!) All this distinctly aids us to the enjoyment of the verses. And poets of our day will find an enjoyment (less unalloyed) in the appended letter of January 7th, from a publisher, enclosing twenty-five dollars for the poem, and promising its appearance "next Saturday."

"My Lost Youth" "came to me" in the night after a day lost in physical pain, and was written next morning (March 30, 1855).

Longfellow was by no means content to live as a lyric poet and sonneteer. We quoted just now the sonnet written by the poet on his thirty-fifth birthday, at Marienberg. The

"Tower of song with lofty parapet,"

which it was his life's highest ambition to raise, was even then beginning to shape itself in his mind. In his notebook appears:

"Christus, a dramatic poem in three parts:
    Part   I.   The Times of Christ. (Hope.)
    Part II. The Middle Ages. (Faith.)
    Part III. The Present. (Charity.)"

This plan he succeeded in executing. The central portion, the "Golden Legend," appeared in 1851, the "New England Tragedies" in 1868, the "Divine Tragedy" in 1871. The next year "Christus, a Mystery," contained the Prelude, Interludes, and Epilogue which complete the work.

But it is not generally accepted in its entirety, by critics or by the general voice, as his masterpiece. The "Golden Legend," to be sure, combines all Longfellow's highest powers, including his mellow, thoughtful scholarship, more adequately than any other single work. The "Divine Tragedy" does not seem to most of us a proper subject for poetic recasting: and, indeed, Longfellow's reverence for the very words of the gospels has hampered his artistic freedom very seriously. I for one would sacrifice it more readily than any other large work of Longfellow. As for the two tragic episodes in early New England life, the witchcraft delusion and the persecution of the Quakers, they are eminently fitted for dramatic treatment. But Longfellow's two plays — like the rest of "Christus" — were unsuited for success on the stage, of which indeed he had little practical knowledge. Nor are they especially typical or illustrative, in any adequate sense, of modern Christianity. Finally, Longfellow is entering in these "tragedies" a field especially associated with Hawthorne's genius; and despite the wide diversity of forms, his inferior dramatic power is made quite evident. He had himself serious misgivings as to "Christus" as a whole, and published the "Divine Tragedy," especially, with little confidence of success.

Upon the whole, the subject attempted in this great trilogy seems too large to be treated within any one frame; much larger, even, than the Promethean myth: and there was nothing of the Titan in Longfellow's nature. The same craving for some monumental accomplishment continued to haunt the poet still. There is a close parallelism here between the latter years of the greatest English poet of the Victorian Age and our own best-beloved singer. And especially persistent was Longfellow's desire to shape an effective drama. In "Michael Angelo," which he was inclined to keep long upon his working table, as a congenial companion of his own old age, we hear through the weary sculptor's lips the poet sighing still of

"The fever to accomplish some great work,
That will not let us sleep. I must go on until I die."

The fact is self-evident that no dramatic masterpiece has ever been produced on American soil. The "Masque of Pandora," I fancy, was never seriously so intended. It is hardly more than a thread just strong enough to hold together the series of lyrics for which it exists: upon which, at least, it must rest its hopes of even partial survival. From "Judas Maccabæus" there remains in the memory only that pathetic figure, the mother of the seven murdered heroes. The "Spanish Student," though not by any means drawn from the utmost depths of the Puritan poet's nature, is a charming idyll of youth and romance. Well may the poet exclaim, in later years:

"How much of my young heart, O Spain,
Went out to thee in days of yore!"

It has never been successfully acted, I believe, but surely Preciosa could be made an effective part, especially for an actress who could dance the Cachuca before the cardinal!

And as our best-beloved poet has here made the nearest approach to a success in dramatic form yet achieved in New England literature, so "Evangeline" and "Hiawatha" are the noblest substitutes we can offer for the great American epic that shall be. They do not, indeed, like the "Iliad" or the "Æneid," embody the triumphant activity of the singer's own race. They do express perfectly our elegiac sympathy for the Anglo-Saxon's vanquished foemen. Of all Longfellow's works, "Hiawatha" is the one wherein the time, the man, and the material united most happily to the creation of a work which else could never have been, and which the world could ill spare. For the sufferings of the Jews, for Mediævalism, for New England witchcraft, for Pandora's youth or Angelo's age, even, perhaps, for Evangeline's pathetic life-story, other poets equally effective might arise hereafter. Some of these themes, indeed, are not finally assured as Longfellow's own. But nearly every one, I think, feels that the romance of the

American Indian has here been crystallized perfectly once for all, and for all time. The theme has even led the poet farther into the heart of the woods than he would else have found his way. Hiawatha's hunting, wooing, canoe-building, have the true fragrance of the aboriginal forest.

Longfellow's poetical work includes experiments in nearly every familiar English metre, as well as in some forms peculiarly his own. For continuous narrative he often uses the four-accent iambic line most familiar from Scott's "Lady of the Lake":

> "The stag at eve had drunk his fill,
> Where danced the moon on Monan's rill."

But he makes the sequence of rhymes so varied, that no tendency to couplet or other stanza is usually felt. He can also vary its speed greatly by the freer introduction of extra syllables. Thus the Prelude and Interludes of the "Wayside Inn" were given a calm, equable flow, wherein

> "A pleasant murmur smote the ear,
> Like water rushing through a weir."

But we all feel it is with nimbler feet that

> "Baron Castine of St. Castine
> Has left his chateau in the Pyrenees,"

and the pace quickened to a long, hard gallop as

> "Through the night rode Paul Revere:
> And through the night went his cry of alarm
> To every Middlesex village and farm."

The slower more regular form of this metre Whittier has borrowed for "Snowbound," which appeared a year or two after the first part of the "Wayside Inn."

The tensyllable heroic couplet, so familiar in elder English verse, Longfellow uses rather after the fashion of Goldsmith, or Chaucer, than of Pope, not clashing each pair of verses like cymbals, but "running on" often from one couplet to the next. This metre is a still greater favorite with Holmes; but no example since the "Deserted Village" seems to me more melodious than "Lady Wentworth" and "King Robert of Sicily." We may perhaps set here a brief passage from the latter poem, as a type of the easy flow and the noble simplicity in Longfellow's most finished masterpieces:

> "And when the angel met him on his way,
> And half in earnest, half in jest, would say,
> Sternly, though tenderly, that he might feel
> The velvet scabbard held a sword of steel,
> 'Art thou the King?' the passion of his woe
> Burst from him in resistless overflow,
> And, lifting high his forehead, he would fling
> The haughty answer back, 'I am, I am the King!'"

The extra foot in the last line of this, and two other stanzas, is an example of Longfellow's accurate feeling for rhythm. Holmes has discussed a more delicate illustration thereof, in the elder poet's Prelude, namely, the regular omission of a syllable in the fifth line of each sextette. The noble poem, "King Robert of Sicily," has a singular interest in connection with what was perhaps the most remarkable of the poet's many friendships. Dom Pedro had a high regard for Longfellow, both as man and minstrel. And among the numerous translations is recorded a version of this poem in Portuguese, by the blameless Brazilian monarch, who was thrust from his own throne at last, — though not by an angel, — no less suddenly and more tragically than the Sicilian tyrant.

The English hexameter was to Longfellow a subject of lifelong interest and study. Besides "Evangeline" and "Miles Standish," there is also a sustained experiment in "Elizabeth" (a Quaker replica of Priscilla), a Tale of the Wayside Inn. A half line therefrom has been recently lifted into notice as the title of "Ships that Pass in the Night." Besides a few minor original poems, some translations in this metre were printed in the poet's lifetime, notably an Eclogue of Virgil, and several of Ovid's Tristia, the latter in elegiac verses. The half-dozen opening lines of the "Iliad," found in the diary, should hardly have been published. They are evidently a casual experiment, wisely abandoned as a failure. Upon the whole, Longfellow has not written as musical hexameters as, for instance, Kingsley or Clough. He seems to me too bold in his disregard of the principle of quantity, which remains in English as a dangerous stumbling-block, at least.

Iambic blank verse, it is generally conceded, becomes in Longfellow's hands, *e.g.* in the "Divine Tragedy," a rather rugged sort of prose. The only great and unquestioned success, indeed, which he scored while free from those fetters of rhyme which he made an ornament and a glory, is the simple, unforced trochaic cradle swing of Hiawatha. This metre, as is well known, was suggested to him from the Finnish Epic of Kalewala; but it was practically unknown in English. So the form, as well as the material, of Hiawatha, makes it the greatest original gift of Longfellow to our literature. There are many single lines which, standing alone, would never suggest the movement, nor indeed, seem like verse at all:

> "As he drew it in it tugged so
> That the birch canoe stood endwise
> Like a birch log in the water."

But the genial easy flow carries along even the heaviest logs of prose.

This beneficent life was prolonged fifteen years beyond that of Hawthorne. All the great tasks which Mr. Longfellow set himself were completed, save the dramatic poem of "Michael Angelo," which he apparently did not desire to lay aside. He suffered no such decay of memory and loss of the power of expression as

Emerson. The wish so beautifully indicated in "Morituri Salutamus," and still more clearly in the motto taken from Horace for "Ultima Thule," was granted to the full. "With mind unbroken," he passed "his age not lacking honor nor the lyre." The gift of song remained to the last. When "Ultima Thule" appeared in 1880, Lowell wrote his friend, "Never was your hand firmer." The beautiful and pathetic sonnet of December, 1881, "To My Books," is still proof of mastery over the most exacting of poetic forms. The last friend to see him in health was Luigi Monti, the "young Italian," of the "Wayside Inn." This was on Saturday, March 18, 1882. That night he became suddenly ill, and lingered less than a week. On March 15 he had written these, his last, tenderly prophetic verses:

> "Out of the shadow of night
> The world rolls into light;
> It is daybreak everywhere."

V

WHITTIER

THE QUAKER LAUREATE OF PURITANISM

It is impossible for a New Englander, whose memories go back to the Civil War and beyond, to assume the attitude of the cold literary critic at the mention of John Greenleaf Whittier's name. A poet born he certainly was, but even his poetic activity was, almost from the beginning, drawn into the full current of that strife against slavery to which he so early and completely devoted himself. Unless some anthology of our bucolic poetry shall chance to outlive for centuries all the records of that gigantic struggle, Whittier will be remembered even more as the trumpet-voice of Emancipation, than as the peaceful singer of rural New England. Indeed, until near his sixtieth year, — when the result so long sought by peaceful means came in the swift whirlwind of war, — he had regarded all hours spent on lighter themes than human freedom as mere self-indulgent diversion.

"The great eventful Present hides the Past; but through the din
Of its loud life, hints and echoes from the life behind steal in;
And the love of home and fireside, and the legendary rhyme,
Makes the task of duty lighter which the true man owes his time." ("Garrison of Cape Ann.")

The "Proem," in particular, marks this devotion of Whittier's life to a moral cause:

"O Freedom! If to me belong
Nor mighty Milton's gift divine,
Nor Marvell's wit and graceful song,
Still with a love as deep and strong
As theirs, I lay, like them, my best gifts on thy shrine!"

And certainly, the Quaker poet of New England had little leisure to polish most of these early offerings laid on Freedom's altar. Often, he says, "They were written with no expectation that they would survive the occasions which called them forth: They were protests, alarm signals, trumpet-calls to action, words wrung from the writer's heart, and, of course, lacking the finish and careful word-selection which reflection and patient brooding over them might have given. Such as they are, they belong to the history of the Anti-slavery movement, and may serve as way-marks of its progress.

Some well-known blemishes on Whittier's verses may often be charged to this headlong haste and fury in composition and publication. A few finished lyrics — notably the "Proem" itself, "Ichabod," the closing hymn in the "Tent on the Beach" — indicate that peaceful leisure, a wider culture, more deliberate habits of composition, would, perhaps, have enabled him to produce more faultless verses.

But it is the general feeling, that few men have had a life better fitted, upon the whole, to reveal and perfect all their highest and rarest gifts. He was not, as he once calls himself, merely "A dreamer born," though the power to dream sweetly was, indeed, part of his intellectual outfit. Yet his keen, lustrous eyes were as evidently and inevitably wide awake from his very childhood, to the efforts for civic and social improvement, — which for true New Englanders is the very inmost essence of real living, — as were those of his deeper-toned kinsman, the defender of the constitution. To the serious business of political life, I say, Whittier's own impulses led as inevitably as Webster's.

Even the voices of strife and violence were sweet in his ears, as the bugle to the war horse. This, indeed, is a contradiction, amid his sincere Quaker convictions and traditions of non-resistance, — a contradiction which caused Whittier much rather whimsical perplexity. "Without intending any disparagement of my peaceable ancestry for many generations," he says, "I have still strong suspicions that somewhat of the old Norman blood, something of the grim Berserker spirit, has been bequeathed to me." His friends thoroughly enjoyed this incongruity, if he did not. Nathaniel Hawthorne's quiet humor is felt in his allusion to the "fiery Quaker youth to whom the Muse has perversely assigned a battle trumpet." And Lowell, who himself was little troubled with scruples about smiting the smiter, cheers on heartily the singer whose

> "Vehement heart
> Strains the strait-breasted drab of the Quaker apart,"

and who leads the fray,

> "Both singing and striking in front of the war,
> And hitting his foes with the mallet of Thor."

Indeed, the early Quakers in New England were not so very remote in spirit from the persecuting but also persecuted Puritans, who used to announce calmly to their English governors their intention to submit, quietly, to injustice — if need be, "*after due and righteous effort to amend it!*" a sort of meekness which their oppressors never enjoyed. It is well to remember that Puritan and Quaker both often sprang, as Whittier indeed has just hinted, from the best Norman or Saxon stock; that courage and fearless devotion to duty were precisely the qualities bred into them both by the fire of persecution; and that the Friends have never sought seclusion, or taken refuge in silence, from the strife of a world wherein they knew other men would fight for conscience' sake, though they might only protest and suffer. But, indeed, in a great moral crisis like our Civil War, the peaceful tenets of Fox have always fallen off from many, even of the devoutest, among the younger Friends, as easily as the drab coat is flung down in the harvest field.

Whittier's gift, in truth, is no such rare flower of genius as that to which Hawthorne rightly devoted a lifetime of seclusion and artistic consecration. His music is nowise unique and inimitable. A certain monotonous simplicity, also, like the voice of his beloved brook, his warmest admirers hardly deny. It has been well said, that his love of home, of humanity, and of God are hardly more than three outpourings from the same source. He often recalls Tennyson's description of

> " Him who sings
> To one clear harp in divers tones."

That it does ring clear and sweet to our Yankee ears, at least, is certain. The misplaced accents, the crude rhymes, are undeniable, to be sure, but even they are usually familiar to the dialect of our own childhood. The Mayflower of our woods is the arbútus to us, whatever the sin against Latin quantity rules, which after all only apply to the name given, in a dead language, to an unfamiliar tree! One jingle (or jangle) in the dear, familiar childish ballad of "Maud Muller" does perhaps set even our teeth on edge. The good gray poet himself must have joined in the laugh, a decade or two agone, when a picturesque, but rather tiresome, old demagogue failed of a reëlection in the Bay State, and the newspapers took up the merry refrain:

"Of all glad words of tongue or pen,
The gladdest are these,—we *shan't have Ben!*"

Yet even this shocking vulgarism—ben for bin, or bean—we have all heard from the lips of our good country aunts, as Hosea Biglow testifies a score of times, *e.g.*:

"Sez he, I'm up to all thet air;
I guess I've *ben* to muster."

(And by the way, it will amuse any true-blue Yankee to learn from the excellent biographer of Lowell, Francis H. Underwood, that "this dialect is essentially extinct!") The contradictions, the limitations, and even the undoubted blemishes, therefore, in Whittier's verse often endear him the more to his fellow-provincials. We love him as the Scots do Burns, because he is just his faulty, glorious self!

Whether Whittier's first American ancestor was actually a Friend or not is doubtful. Probably not, since he held civic and even military positions. He certainly sympathized with some of the Quaker tenets. He refused to own firearms, or even to bar his house against the Indians, who were often heard whispering under his windows in the night, but never molested his family, — even when the atrocities of savage warfare filled the Merrimac valley with terror. In that picturesque region the family has won a toilsome but independent livelihood from the soil for two centuries and a half. The old homestead immortalized in "Snowbound" still stands, a few miles from Haverhill, shut in by rolling hills from sight of all other human habitations. It has been purchased recently as a permanent memorial of the poet. I was delighted at my first glimpse from the road, upon a snowy day, when a horse in the old barn pushed forth his face to greet us, just as eighty years ago

> "The old horse thrust his long head out,
> And grave with wonder gazed about."

Those earlier Whittiers do not appear to have been impelled to bear testimony against the vanities of seventeenth-century Puritanism in a form which brought down upon them the sharpest edge of persecution. Possibly in these bleak Northern hills there was never such magnificence in steeple-house edifices, splendor of priestly robes, or other sinful luxuries as were a grievous offence in Boston-on-the-Bay!

Of the simplest and hardiest farmer life "Snowbound," "In Schooldays," "My Playmate," "Barefoot Boy," and other personal poems give an absolutely truthful picture. This was really Whittier's boyhood; and his early life was much humbler than that of all our other poets. But it has been wisely pointed out, that the comparison of "Snowbound" to the "Cotter's Saturday Night," or Whittier's own allusion to "these Flemish pictures of old days," is in one very large respect inexact. The circle about the New England winter fire are not peasants; certainly they have never thought of recognizing any earthly master. Money was scarce, and books were few indeed. But at least the newspapers kept them in touch with the great outside world. In the local councils and town offices the Whittiers had an honorable share. In their own narrow, quiet, uneventful world they had no superiors.

In the little district schoolhouse, half a mile away, the boy Whittier spent the three winter months of each year, the instructor being usually himself a boy or youth, fresh from college, — if indeed yet graduated. Of the twenty-odd volumes in the homestead, the nearest approach to poetry was the one in which

> "Ellwood's meek drab-skirted muse,
> A stranger to the heathen Nine,
> Sang, with a somewhat nasal whine,
> The wars of David and the Jews."

This dismal "Davideis" does not seem to have inspired the boy, though there is a record of his remark, that the warrior king could not have been a good Friend! This, however, may be rather a reminiscence of the First Day afternoons spent happily with his mother over the Old and New Testament, with which his own works show a perfect familiarity.

But a happy chance soon put into his hands the one book of all others best fitted to open his eyes to the beauty in common things. Whittier himself tells the story, in a delightful and humorous little prose essay on "Yankee Gypsies." The tramps of that day were less numerous, and more varied and picturesque, if not more deserving, than now. "One day," says Whittier, "we had a call from a 'pawky auld carle' of a wandering Scotchman. To him I owe my first introduction to the songs of Burns. After eating his bread and cheese, and drinking his mug of cider, he gave us 'Bonnie Doon,' 'Highland Mary,' and 'Auld Lang Syne.'" Later performances to which Whittier had listened "lacked," as he says, "the novel charm of the gaberlunzie's singing in the old farmhouse kitchen." Later, when the boy was fourteen, his first schoolmaster, Joshua Coffin, — afterward his fellow-abolitionist, — gave him a copy of Burns' poems, and helped him to master the dialect. In his own earliest attempts at rhyme, which are probably all lost, he even imitated the Scotticisms of Burns. But the real benefit of that gift he expresses in his own verses on the Scotch poet:

> "With clearer eyes I saw the worth
>   Of life among the lowly.
> The Bible at his Cotter's hearth
>   Had made my own more holy.
>
> "Why dream of lands of gold and pearl,
>   Of loving Knight and Lady,
> When farmer boy and barefoot girl
>   Were wandering there already?"

To Burns Whittier owes, at least, the first clear apprehension of that elemental rule of the artist which Longfellow has perhaps preached better than he has practised it:

> "That is best which lieth nearest:
>   Shape of that thy work of art."

Whittier learned, with Burns' help, to count his treasures aright.

"I was rich in flowers and trees,
  Humming-birds and honey-bees;
For my sport the squirrel played,
Plied the snouted mole his trade;
For my taste the blackberry cone
Purpled over hedge and stone;
Laughed the brook for my delight
Through the day and through the night,
Whispering at the garden wall,
Talked with me from fall to fall;
Mine the sand-rimmed pickerel pond,
Mine the walnut slopes beyond, . . .
Still as my horizon grew,
Larger grew my riches too;
All the world I saw or knew
Seemed a complex Chinese toy,
Fashioned for a barefoot boy!"

At nineteen, Whittier was a tall, slender, keen-eyed but shy farmer-boy, hoeing industriously in the corn-field, — barefooted often, still, — or perhaps poring over a book at the winter fire. His rhymes had not, apparently, turned his own thoughts, nor those of his kin, to a different career than that of his ancestry. But again, as in the gift of Burns' poems, the right spark fell into the quiet, eager young life.

William Lloyd Garrison, himself only three years Whittier's senior, but already devoted at heart to some of the reforms which were to constitute the work of his life, established a paper, the "Free Press," in Newburyport. To him some of Whittier's verses had been sent by a sister, apparently without the writer's knowledge. The Whittiers had subscribed for the paper, "liking its humanitarian tone," and the young poet has recorded his delighted surprise when the number containing his own verses was tossed over the fence from the stage into the field where he was at work.

Not many days after he was summoned in haste from his work on the farm. A visitor had driven up to the house — a rare event. It was the eager young editor, who came to persuade the cautious father that so promising a poetic talent demanded higher education and encouragement. The opportunity came, in humble guise indeed! Whittier learned the shoemaker's art, in its simplest and crudest form, from a laborer on the farm, and earned enough during the winter to spend six months at the new Haverhill academy. He wrote the ode for the dedication of the building (verses which have utterly perished), and immediately won his master's admiring regard, especially by his prose essays. In the six months' term he made remarkable progress in English studies, and learned some French. An unhappy and brief experience as teacher won him the means for a second term at the academy.

With this slender preparation, Whittier almost instantly began an active career as editor and writer. His verses, in particular, were readily published and admired from the first. He never had a struggle for recognition. On the contrary, it is difficult to understand what he had written, for instance, by his twenty-second year, that inspired the prophecy quoted in the "New England Review" (December, 1829): "The culmination of that man's fame will be a proud period in the history of our literature." Nearly all the verses of this period have been carefully suppressed by the maturer taste of the poet. There is one passage, rescued against his will, that gives a vivid impression of his ambitious energy in these years, and also of his early devotion to patriotic duty:

> "Land of my fathers! if the name,
> Now humble and unused to fame,

> Hereafter burn upon the lip
> As one of those which may not die,
> Linked in eternal fellowship
> With visions pure, and strong, and high,—
> If the wild dreams which quicken now
> The thrilling pulse of heart and brow
> Hereafter take a real form,
> Like spectres changed to beings warm,
> And over temples worn and gray
> The star-like crown of glory shine,
> Thine be the bard's undying lay,
> The murmur of his praise be thine!"

Here we have already, at twenty-two, the chief keys of Whittier's verse clearly struck. The dangerous fluency and facility, the choice of a somewhat obvious — occasionally even of a hackneyed — adjective, he never fully escaped. The pure aspiration, the clear, straightforward vigorous expression, the easy rapid movement of the rhythm, everything save the freer expression, in this early time, of his own hopes and desires, would admit these youthful rhymes, without a jar, into a page of "Snowbound," or "Tent on the Beach."

We naturally seek, among an author's earlier poems, for verses on the subject whereunto "a young man's fancy lightly turns." Whittier, alone, among our great poets and literary men generally, never married. The reasons for this have never, so far as I know, been fully revealed. He was in no sense misanthropic, still less misogynic, and seems to have been remarkably fitted to make any true-hearted woman happy. Nor is there any substantial trace of an early disappointment in love. It seems to me not unlikely, that he made a silent, lifelong sacrifice to the home happiness of his mother and sisters. This he himself intimates in his correspondence. There is apparently no adequate evidence that this decision cost him a very bitter pang on any especial occasion. That a single life is a sacrifice, or a loss, we hear often echoed, as when the dear maiden aunt is described,

> "The sweetest woman ever Fate
> Perverse denied a household mate."

The feminine element is indeed very pervasive throughout "Snowbound." Not only is this true of the central domestic picture, but in the larger village background. "At every house," as the teams break a way along the snow-laden road,

> "the watchful young men saw
> Sweet doorway pictures of the curls
> And curious eyes of merry girls."

And near the beginning of "Yankee Gypsies" is an unexpected bit of Oriental color, where we see "bright eyes glancing above the uplifted muff, like a sultana's behind the folds of her *yashmak*." Doubtless, however, it was his Quaker soul-brother Bayard Taylor who brought this word and this glimpse back to the homekeeping poet.

Evidence for authentic love-making of Whittier's own begins "In Schooldays," at about the age of seven, with the tender words:

> "'I'm sorry that I spelt the word,
> I hate to go above you,
> Because,' the brown eyes lower fell,
> 'Because, you see, I love you!'"

And the same refrain is repeated at the close of the little poem, in a saddened minor key very rarely heard in Whittier's verse:

> "He lives to learn, in life's hard school,
> How few who pass above him

> Lament their triumph and his loss,
> Like her, — because they love him!"

But this little sweetheart, probably the daughter of a near neighbor, upon whose grave the grasses of forty years had blown, cannot be the same as "My Playmate," who at the last parting

> "Kist the lips of kith and kin"

but

> "laid her hand in mine:
> What more could ask the bashful boy
> Who fed her father's kine?"

This later child-love passes, in the poem, to a long and prosperous life in the Southland. There may be some real hint here, and elsewhere, of an early regard for a woman who perhaps then seemed above him in social station. The striking references in "Memories" are clearly to a woman, still living, whom he had known and held dear as a schoolboy (perhaps at twenty):

> "I hear again thy low replies,
>   I feel thy arm within my own,
> And timidly again uprise
> The fringed lids of hazel eyes,
>   With soft brown tresses overblown."

The definiteness of the "local color," in iris and hair, indicates realism! Whittier would hardly have accepted Emerson's mystical apophthegm, that the truly blest lover "Loveth downward, and not up!" At threescore and ten he gave expression to the opposite sentiment in "The Henchman," which might perhaps bear the excision of several among its eleven quatrains, — yet every one adds force to the single thought:

> "The love that no return doth crave
> To knightly level lifts the slave."

Yet there seems to be a trace of evidence, that the longing for a full return of earthly love demanded utterance at last, though age and death had made it doubly impossible. The effort to envelope it, as it were, under an alien address only convinces one reader, at least, that the song in "A Sea Dream" is that saddest utterance, the memory of what might have been, from a heart that has never ceased to feel the loneliness of solitude. It is not a guardian angel to whom he cries; but the wife he never won:

> "But turn to me thy dear girl-face
> Without the angel's crown,
> The wedded roses of thy lips,
> Thy loose hair rippling down
> In waves of golden brown."

Yet this is undoubtedly all we shall ever know or guess.

> "He came and went, and left no sign
> Behind him save the song he sung."

These closing words are plainly intended to baffle our own curious gaze after him. (Since these sentences were written some very positive and definite statements have been published in regard to Whittier's youthful attachment; but those best able to speak are forever silent, and never meant to leave a clearer sign behind them. Far be it from me to tear away the veil they drew.)

We have followed, too far afield perhaps, a path which leads no-whither; but the fact that a man so gentle, so sympathetic, yet so ardent, walked alone all his days, is really interesting, and might be in some sense a key to character: or, at least, the cause for some of his artistic limitations, since he confessedly missed the happier and richer inner side of life! But my immediate purpose was to lead toward a phase of his poetry which is less often noticed.

If the question of slavery and the Abolition agitation had never invaded our life, Whittier's career might have been as tranquil and changeless as the full current of the Merrimac by which he dwelt. His poetry would at least have been a faithful echo of the familiar sounds, and a mirror for the hills and lakes, of his beloved New England.

Of such poetry from him we have, as it is, perhaps an adequate mass. The rather scanty legends of the Eastern coast he sought out and versified, as in the "Wreck of the Palatine." Others, notably a favorite of boyhood, "Amy Wentworth," he invented for himself. Of his "Songs of Labor," the "Huskers" and the "Shoemakers" in particular are transcripts from his own early memories. We need not dwell on this side of his life-work, because its results are quite as popular, to say the least, as they deserve; and also because his experience uplifted him to higher levels of verse.

The influence of Garrison had an important part, as we have seen, in making Whittier a better educated young man, an author by profession, and thereby, at first in a very humble way, an editor. These latter duties were indeed often combined or alternated with hard work upon the Haverhill farm.

As to the cause which was already the main purpose of Garrison's life, Whittier did not at once take his stand. To be an Abolitionist meant social and political ostracism, scorn, probably persecution. Whittier was peculiarly sensitive to ridicule, fond of approval, throbbing with literary ambition. He did not, perhaps, hesitate as to duty, when the duty was clear to him; but he did weigh the matter well, and count the cost. He thought he might go unflinching to the stake, if need be; but was sure he could never wear with dignity the coat of tar and feathers! Yet his final decision in 1833, five years after Garrison took his decisive stand, was equally irrevocable. In June of that year, he published his vigorous prose pamphlet, "Justice and Expediency: or, Slavery Considered with a View to Its Rightful and

Effectual Remedy, Abolition." This at once gave Whittier a leading place in the advanced ranks of Emancipationists. Soon after he printed, in the "Haverhill Gazette," his famous lines to Garrison, loyally hailing him as his chief, "Champion of those who groan beneath oppression's iron hand."

This leadership of Garrison Whittier never ceased to acknowledge, and he has declared that he took more pride in his name among the sixty-two signatures to the Declaration of Principles, drafted by Garrison in December, 1833, when the American Antislavery Society was founded in Philadelphia, than in any literary achievement. (See Whittier's reminiscences in the "Atlantic Monthly" for February, 1874.)

But it will be remembered that a great rift opened between the Garrisonian abolitionists, who abstained from all political action, — who would even gladly have broken up the Union to escape all connection with slaveholders, — and the founders of the Liberal party, later merged into the Free Soil movement, and finally in the Republican organization. These latter sought the limitation and eventual abrogation of slavery by peaceful, political, and constitutional action. To this less violent wing of abolitionism Whittier's judgment led him, and for fifteen years (1839–1854) Garrison regarded him — most intolerantly — almost as a renegade from the cause. From 1854 onward, to the full triumph of 1863, they were again in harmony personally, and to a great extent in their methods of work. Throughout the earlier struggle, of course, Whittier's fiery lyrics were copied everywhere — even into the "Liberator." Indeed, they were at each fresh crisis the clearest voice of the fast-growing Northern sentiment against slavery.

Among the earliest poems of this period, the "Song of the Kansas Emigrants" was a household word in that unhappy Border State, and indeed actually the marching song of the westward pilgrim trains:

> "We cross the prairie, as of old
> The pilgrims crossed the sea,
> To make the West, as they the East,
> The homestead of the free!"

Perhaps the most familiar and unforgettable of all is "Massachusetts to Virginia":

> "The blast from Freedom's Northern hills, upon its southern way,
> Bears greeting to Virginia from Massachusetts Bay."

There is the sure prescience of final victory in such lines as the closing verses:

> "No slave hunt in our borders, — no pirate on our strand!
> No fetters in the Bay State, — no slave upon our land!"

The masterpiece among Whittier's political lyrics is, however, without question, "Ichabod." This terrible winged arrow of reproof was written in 1850, after Whittier's distant kinsman, Daniel Webster, had made that famous seventh of March speech of conciliation, or surrender, the moral significance of which is still under discussion. Surely no man has the right to pass such merciless judgment on another. The culmination seems actually Dantesque in its very thought:

> "Of all we loved and honored, naught
> Save power remains, —
> A fallen angel's pride of thought,
> Still strong in chains.
>
> "All else is gone; from those great eyes
> The soul has fled;

> When faith is lost, when honor dies,
> The man is dead!"
>
> (*Cf.* "Inferno," XXXIII, 121–135.)

Whittier never retracted these fearful words directly, but his personal feeling toward Webster softened greatly with the years. Toward the end of his life he wrote "The Lost Occasion," which he set beside "Ichabod," — quite out of chronological order, — in the final edition of his works. Here he expresses the fullest confidence that Webster, if he had lived to see the Civil War, would have been foremost to urge on the North. There is even a clinging personal regard, that almost forgets resignation to Heaven's will, in the words:

> "Ah, cruel fate, that closed to thee,
> O sleeper by the Northern sea,
> The gates of opportunity!"

A part of the compromise to which Webster gave his assent on this famous occasion was the Fugitive Slave Law. The comparatively few attempts to enforce this law in Northern States manufactured antislavery sentiment faster than almost anything else. Upon those who urged submission to it as a duty of good citizenship, Whittier poured all the vials of scorn and contempt. "A Sabbath Scene," for instance, has a caustic fire, a rough dramatic power, that carries it safely off over such rhymes as *figure* and *eager, glided* and "*strided,*" *teacher* and *nature, stumbling* and *trembling*.

As for the John Brown episode in our history, Whittier celebrated in striking verses the incident of Brown's kissing the negro child on his march to the gallows. The contest as to the real occurrence of this incident we need not touch upon. But there is, in this poem, a curious bit of evidence against the popular feeling that Whittier was the inspired prophet, as well as poet, of Freedom. The pious prayer,

"Nevermore may yon blue ridges the Northern rifle hear,"

must remind us that, only twenty months later, countless regiments were marching southward, to the swinging refrain of "John Brown's Body," for a war whose bloodiest battles were to redden Virginian soil.

During the war itself, the heart of the patriot

and reformer throbbed fierce and hot against the strait-waistcoat of the Quaker. How he *ought* to feel he tells us, *e.g.* in the "Anniversary Poem," written for an audience of Friends in 1863. But "The Summons" has certainly another sound:

> "Shamed be the hands that idly fold,
>   And lips that woo the reed's accord,
>   When laggard Time the hour has tolled
>   For true with false and new with old
>   To fight the battles of the Lord!"

He repines, even, if I read the words aright, at the physical weakness which alone will keep him from the tented field:

> "To him your summons comes too late
>   Who sinks beneath his armor's weight,
>   And has no answer but God-speed!"

To a certain grim delight taken by Whittier, in spite of himself, in valorous battle (for a righteous cause, be it well understood!), we have already alluded, and many illustrations could be accumulated. Of course, it is not the savage glee in strife itself that we feel so often in the Homeric fray or the battles of the Nibelungen. Still, in the best of all Whittier's ballads upon remoter themes, the "Pipes at Lucknow," we are not told to shudder at the crisis, when

> "The tartan clove the turban,
> As the Goomtee cleaves the plain."

The reversion to peaceful tasks produced almost instantaneously, as it seemed, Whittier's most popular and probably most permanent work. "Snowbound" appeared in 1865, just after the close of the war. This poem has been universally accepted as the absolutely truthful and final picture of country life in New England. There is hardly a word in it indicating that the Quaker household felt itself in any respect apart from the other elements of the community. The "Inner Light" of trust and hope which brightens the saddest memories of change and loss is but the common faith of humanity, the voice of conscience. By this poem, we firmly believe, Whittier's name will live as long as the influence of New England itself is remembered among men.

Only in a single passage does the problem of the hour disturb the idyllic contemplation of the past. After describing the boyish schoolmaster, the poet digresses, in rather forced fashion:

> ". . . of such as he
> Shall Freedom's young apostles be,
> Who, following in War's bloody trail,
> Shall every lingering wrong assail." . . .

There are twenty-five lines here which could be spared. And the reformer's conscience is still not easy in his brief repose. At the last,

> "I hear again the voice that bids
> The dreamer leave his dream midway,
> For larger hopes and graver fears."

On the whole, however, Whittier's poetic art, like his reformer's career, had now culminated, though much that is of permanent value and charm may doubtless be culled from his later as from his earlier work. The process of winnowing the wheat from the chaff will in his case be a severe and seemingly cruel task of time. Not only whole poems of transitory value or meaning, but many a weak, incongruous stanza, even from lyrics of lasting beauty, will doubtless fall away silently with the years. Thus, when Charles Sumner died, Longfellow (of whom Emerson, in his turn, complained that he "wrote too much") gathered up a little handful of his choicest and purest gems, and produced a glistening mosaic of only thirty-six briefest lines, worthy to be reproduced and eternalized in letters of gold upon monumental marble. Whittier published his tribute in just *six times* as many verses! Yet the author of "Ichabod" should have known better the limits of lyric effectiveness. In the stead of these many stanzas, *eight* of the two hundred and sixteen lines alone would have been, to my mind, a loftier and more enduring tribute:

> "God said: 'Break thou these yokes; undo
> These heavy burdens. I ordain
> A work to last thy whole life through,
> A ministry of strife and pain.
>
> .
>
> "'Forego thy dreams of lettered ease,
> Put thou the scholar's promise by,
> The rights of men are more than these.'
> He heard, and answered: 'Here am I!'"

But, indeed, Whittier himself has winnowed his early poems, at least, with a severity which in some instances we feel to be excessive. Thus from July, 1830, to the end of the next year, while editing the "New England Review," he made forty poetical contributions, of which only *three* are taken up into the final revised edition of 1888. Still, an exhaustive study of all this youthful work would not be enjoyable or profitable, as in the case of Hawthorne, since so much of it was hastily turned off — and also because Whittier never attained any such remarkable mastery of form as the author of the "Gray Champion" and the "Scarlet Letter."

There are still three features of Whittier's best work to which I wish in closing to call especial attention.

In the first place, the accurate yet idealized description of natural scenery. This is a constant characteristic of his earliest as of his latest writings. He is far too modest in the "Proem":

> "Unskilled the subtle lines to trace,
>   Or softer shades of Nature's face,
>   I view her common forms with unanointed eyes."

On the contrary, those thoughtful men and women who are most familiar with the scenes amid which he dwelt in lifelong content, find themselves, often indeed, gazing in memory upon them, as it were, through Whittier's eyes. The best single illustration of this is a poem which is to many, perhaps, as familiar and as dear as "Snowbound" itself: the "Last Walk in Autumn." This seems to me to claim a high artistic merit; and a deeper harmony of music and meditative pathos than usual haunts even such quiet lines as:

"And scarlet berries tell where bloomed the sweet wild-rose."

Indeed, to a stranger we might be tempted to offer this, rather than "Snowbound" itself, first of all, as convincing evidence that our Quaker laureate of Puritan New England is a far-sighted and aspiring artist. The charm of foreign journeying has rarely been more thrillingly sung than by this home-keeping minstrel, though he begins:

"I know not how, in other lands,
The changing seasons come and go."

It chances that these same stanzas offer equally good illustrations of the other two traits to which I undertook to call attention. One is his close and tender attachment to his friends. The tributes to Emerson, to Bayard Taylor, to Charles Sumner, form three noble strophes of the "Last Walk." Taylor again appears, with James T. Fields, in the "Tent on the Beach." There is still a third poem, an early one, dedicated to Sumner, entitled "To C. S." Taylor's death called out a series of three sonnets: a form Whittier rarely essayed. A large number of his works took the form of direct addresses to his friends, or to men he admired, at the crises of their fate. For example:

> "Thy error, Fremont, simply was to act
>   A brave man's part, without the statesmen's tact," etc.

One of the brightest and happiest of these personal tributes, not reprinted, I think, in most editions, is "How Mary Grew." It is a memorial of an heroic woman who was still living until 1897, in Philadelphia, Miss Mary Grew. In old age, Holmes and Whittier, in particular, have often exchanged melodious greetings.

But thirdly, and lastly, we must turn to a side of Whittier's poetry which has always appealed to the heart of universal humanity. I mean the *hymns* in which he utters, so simply and clearly as hardly any other has done, a perfect trust in and resignation to the power that guides our earthly ways aright. A cheerful optimism is indeed characteristic, as was said, of all our New England poets. Each might have uttered Lowell's words:

> "For me Fate gave, whate'er she else denied,
> A nature sloping to the southern side."

Longfellow's last written line is no less bright with hope and trust. Emerson's lyrics fly heavenward, like homing pigeons. Yet in the expression of religious faith and truthfulness Whittier has no rival among them. And here, at least, we account his absolute simplicity among the highest of poetic virtues.

It is not possible to indicate adequately our real feeling in regard to certain utterances of Whittier without allusion to a personal experience. It befell that the dear comrade of many a wide-ranging pilgrimage, a close and faithful sharer in joys and sorrows, lay tranquilly awaiting the final parting. No physical distress save weakness overshadowed the last weeks. From that peaceful upper chamber went forth winged thoughts of unselfish helpfulness and eager interest for numberless friends. Even the rich intellectual life glowed long with steady though quiet flame. But in the last few days, while there was no clouding of the mind, its needs grew slighter, like those of the body, until only the craving for music and for devotional poetry remained. And last of all, down to a time when life itself could only be counted by hours, "My Psalm," the "Eternal Goodness," and the nameless hymn at the close of "Tent on the Beach" were still asked for again and again. As Tennyson doubtless crossed the bar with his own lyric of unquestioning trust to cheer him on his way, — so as pure, gentle and brave a soul as I ever knew passed, almost happily, out of consciousness, with the murmured words as it were still upon the lips:

> "I know not where His islands lift
>   Their fronded palms in air;
> I only know I cannot drift
>   Beyond His love and care."

And so, in one sadly broken circle, at least, these and other lines of Whittier's will always be something nearer and more precious than mere poetic words.

It was not a part of our purpose to trace fully the outward life of Whittier, which has been, in a sense, uneventful. That is, there have been no marked changes in his circumstances which have had a vital effect upon his work. He was more of a politician than is generally supposed, in a generation when politics were perhaps more largely vitalized than now with moral motives and efforts. In 1835 and 1836 he even sat in the state legislature. He was in Philadelphia in May, 1838, when a mob burned Pennsylvania Hall, then just erected by the Antislavery Society. His paper, the "Pennsylvania Freeman," was also burnt out, but he continued its publication for a year longer, when illness compelled his return to Haverhill.

He was for many years poor, and his pen won him very slender returns. The old homestead was sold in 1840, and from that time onward Whittier's legal residence was in the neighboring town of Amesbury. It is as "Hermit of Amesbury" that he is addressed in one of Longfellow's latest sonnets, "The Three Silences." From 1847–1857 he was "corresponding editor" of the "Washington National Era," in which "Uncle Tom's Cabin" first appeared (1851). It contained, too, many of Whittier's finest poems, and also the best of his prose work. Especially notable was "Margaret Smith's Journal," a series of careful pictures from seventeenth-century New England life, with a rather slight thread of plot and incident.

Perhaps 1857 is the year of Whittier's fully assured literary success. In this year his collected poems appeared, and he was invited into the little circle of leading poets of freedom and other literary men, who founded the "Atlantic Monthly." The time of poverty and obscurity was over, and the very name of Abolitionist was soon to become a title of honor.

Whittier's old age was clouded by few sorrows, after the loss of his two sisters, so tenderly recorded in "Snowbound." With this poem he won in an instant the heart of every New Englander. He lived on for nearly thirty years after the war, amid a generation that delighted to honor the Abolitionists, whom their fathers had denounced, mobbed, almost hanged. As he himself says, the voice of fault-finding grew rare indeed.

> "Love watches o'er my quiet ways,
> Kind voices speak my name,
> And lips that find it hard to praise
> Are slow, at least, to blame."

Discussions as to Barbara Frietchie's actual existence, complaints that he had painted Floyd Ireson too black, and the women of Marblehead as too savage, demands from the Block Islanders that the visiting pirates, not the resident wreckers, should be credited with the plundering of the Palatine generations ago, — such pigmy assaults might well make the scarred veteran cry:

> "Methinks the spirit's temper grows
> Too soft in this still air!"

Surrounded by loving friends, fearless, tranquil, indeed only glad to enter into his rest, he bade farewell to earth, after eighty-five years of fearless devotion to his brother-men, in September, 1892.

VI

LOWELL

POET AND PATRIOT

THE stately pair of volumes entitled "Letters of James Russell Lowell," carefully edited in 1893 by Professor Norton, is one of the most valuable books of its class. The departed poet was most fortunate in his editor. Everything which would merely gratify an impertinent curiosity has been quietly pruned away. But even then, as Mr. Norton says of his friend, "his poems and his letters show him with rare completeness as he truly was." Herein the editor was fortunate as well. From this rich mass of autobiographic material I shall, necessarily, draw freely. But it is a book which should be *read*, entire, without haste. With Lowell's poems and essays, it would alone suffice for a year or two of earnest profitable study; better, doubtless, than the works of any other one American man of letters. It should be republished in a less monumental and costly form.

Lowell had some advantages not enjoyed by any of the writers we have already discussed: including this, that their young manhood coincided with his childhood, so that he entered largely into the fruits of their labors. The other five most popular New England authors were all born in the first ten years of our century. Lowell's birth falls near the close of the second decade, on February 22, 1819. (This coincidence with Washington's anniversary, by the way, is used with effect by George William Curtis, in that eloquent oration upon his old friend, which was so nearly his own swan-song.) The birth of New England's other most gifted child, Nathaniel Hawthorne, on the fourth of July, seems a more whimsical stroke of chance. Holmes' birth, in the shadow of Harvard and on Commencement Day, appears unmistakably providential in its fitness. Though outlived for several years by two members of the illustrious group, Lowell yet belongs in many ways to the next generation after them all. His early manhood was passed under the healthier conditions, healthier certainly for scholarship and literature, at least, which they were aiding so largely to bring about.

Toward Emerson, especially, his senior by sixteen years, Lowell always takes the attitude of a loyally grateful though independent disciple. "Emerson awakened us, saved us from the body of this death. It is the sound of the trumpet that the young soul longs for, careless what breath may fill it. Sidney heard it in 'Chevy Chase,' and we in Emerson." These words refer to a time when Lowell was an eager boy in his 'teens, while Emerson was already "midway in life's journey." The entire paper ("Emerson the Lecturer") renders full thanks for a continuous debt through more than thirty years since then.

For Hawthorne, also, who was born the year after Emerson, Lowell had the utmost admiration, saying, by implication, that no man had more deeply impressed him "with the constant presence of that indefinable thing we call genius" (Introduction to "Biglow Papers," Second Series). And he intimates elsewhere, that Hawthorne is our one great story-teller, worth forty Boccaccios. (In "Fitz Adams' Story.")

Lowell, then, stands from his boyhood upon a vantage which Emerson and Longfellow had aided in winning for him — and he does honor to his masters. With much of Emerson's idealism, and something of his mysticism as well, (Lowell's keener sense of humor and his warmer temperament kept his feet more firmly and constantly planted upon our earth. His scholarship, too, ploughed much deeper than Longfellow's eclectic Humanism, as the essays on Dante, Chaucer, the Trouvères, etc., suffice to show.)

He took a delight at least as deep as theirs in the scholar's "illuminate seclusion" of industrious ease; and yet he was early forced into far more practical relations than they ever had with contemporary life. It was, indeed, already a life more deeply stirred by moral struggle than that of the earlier agricultural and conservative New England in which Whittier, Hawthorne, and others had approached maturity.

Mr. Norton says, though I do not at all understand him, that after Jackson's administration no more such men could be born.

It seems, at any rate, clear, that no patriotic young American could escape the rude interruption of his scholastic or artistic career by the great struggle for the national life, which was to culminate in civil war. Longfellow might pay his tribute once for all to Emancipation, and return to his study; Hawthorne might touch lightly on slavery, in his life of Pierce, as an evil to be endured in patience until divinely removed in some way as yet inscrutable; but Lowell was of a more aggressive generation. The time came, indeed, when even the dreamer Hawthorne found that his thoughts must busy themselves "Chiefly about War Matters." Lowell, certainly, had quite too much of Milton's and Marvell's Puritan temper to seclude himself an hour longer among his books, when to every patriot had come

"the moment to decide,
In the strife of Truth with Falsehood, for the good or evil
  side."

And that moment arrived for him, when at twenty he came to realize that the Abolitionists *must be heard;* those Abolitionists whom he had just been ridiculing in the graduation poem. (Cf. p. 209.)

Perhaps most men will ascribe the difference between Lowell's life and that of his neighbors and friends, — Emerson, Longfellow, Hawthorne, Holmes, — to his own eager, impetuous nature, rather than to age or circumstances: and there is, at least, some truth in that view. Clearly he had far less of docile receptivity, as a scholar, than Longfellow. We can hardly imagine him a patient translator, year after year, even of the "Commedia." And he accepted little, indeed, of Emerson's calm, contemplative outlook on human existence.

When Hosea Biglow, a youth of twenty-eight only, leaped into the political discussion of the Mexican war time, no one called him a dreamer, though some harder names were used; and almost ever since, indeed long before, one "scholar in politics" has been very much in evidence. As a politician, in the best sense of that much-abused word, he was alert, practical, and wise: though always with a longing eye turned back toward his proper pursuits. Emerson's essay on "Politics" is an abstract treatise, with some applications to current events, or rather conditions. But Lowell's paper in 1860, entitled "The Election in November," was written for the definite purpose of aiding Abraham Lincoln's candidacy: though it, too, is certainly not lacking in appeals to eternal moral principles. This essay is, moreover, in Lowell's collected works, but one in a goodly group of similar papers and orations, which might have been still increased.

Even amid the turmoil of a Republican national convention, Lowell's personal address and conversational persuasiveness once aided, materially, in defeating a nomination regarded by him and his friends as suicidal. Only his absence from the country, in a great diplomatic office, prevented him from sharing with his friend Curtis in the second similar triumph within his party, and in a third less successful struggle,—as well as in the famous "Mugwump" revolt from party allegiance that followed.

When Hawthorne, in 1853, took the lucrative Liverpool consulship, it was solely because this would bring him the financial independence which his genius had failed to win. Though hailed with delight by Sumner as the "one bright spot" in Pierce's administration, the appointment was widely criticised as a barefaced repayment for the reluctant campaign biography. But when Lowell was sent to England, though he was welcomed by "Punch" as the Ambassador of American Literature to the court of St. James, it was generally accepted here at home — as was his earlier mission to Spain — as the rare selection of the one fittest man for the post.

Whatever the cause, then, whether in the man or the circumstances, it seems plain that Lowell's career does illustrate, as no other has yet done, the costly tribute paid by the highest American scholarship and literary power to our political life. He did not, indeed, sacrifice his career as an author to any such extent as his friend, George William Curtis, gave up belles-lettres for journalism, and for the public causes he served so effectively through that channel. But there was, nevertheless, a real sacrifice, more real in his case than in Mr. Curtis', however adequate the compensation may have been. He who sang so stoutly "by the embers of loss I count my gain," would hardly have indulged, without good reason, in serious repining over the work interrupted by the calls to patriotic duty. Yet the private letters of the youthful Abolitionist, of the learned professor, of the ambassador, are full of complaint against all which had distracted him from verse. For instance, as he enters his seventieth year, he says, with all earnestness: "A poet shouldn't be, nay, he can't be, anything else, without loss to him as poet: however much he may gain as man." Of course, this must not be construed with slavish literalness. Our poets cannot be hermits nor monks. Still, of Lowell the writer far more than of any contemporary, it is constantly said: The man was far greater than all the memorials he has left of himself. They do not adequately reveal his genius.

This is probably quite true; and yet it is no final measure for the usefulness of his life. The thousands who heard his "Commemoration Ode," or the anniversary address, at Harvard, realized how the whole man multiplied — for the living hearers at least, and doubtless through them for the after time as well — the force and value of the wingèd words.

The Outward Life

Lowell's father was himself a distinguished clergyman and scholar, a lesser member of the Channing group. That odor of old Russia leather bindings, the familiarity with ponderous folios as the building-blocks of infancy, which the Autocrat thinks so desirable, were among Lowell's earliest impressions: though not earlier than the murmur of the wind in the stately elms and ash trees, or the "mystical cry" of the herons, that still build in the Elmwood thickets, and nowhere else for miles around. This fine old estate of Elmwood, a mile beyond the college gate, and under the slope of Mount Auburn, was his home from birth. Earlier members of the race had been planted, like the forbears of Longfellow and Whittier, in the Merrimac valley: at Newbury. In "Cambridge Thirty Years Ago" (a date which would strictly point to the precocious poet's *fifth* year) is a delicious picture of the quiet old suburban village and all its quaint "characters." In "Under the Willows" is a most tender picture of the poet's immediate surroundings.

Two lifelong passions, for books and for outdoor sights and sounds, took root with life itself. As a Sophomore of seventeen, he writes lovingly of his own new Milton in calf binding, of an English Coleridge just given him by his father, and of the eight-volume octavo of Shakspeare, for which he hopes to afford fourteen dollars "next month." This inclination to spend his next month's income, especially for a rare book, was also lifelong.

But just about the same time, his earliest extant verses are addressed, in genuine affection, to "Our Old Horse Chestnut Tree." They are, it may be added, quite free from the pedantic stiffness and insincerity of most boyish verses. Lines like

> "And thou hast heard our merry shout
> (My brother Bob and I)"

have a truthful ring. We can well believe

that, rocking in its boughs, these keen-eyed boys had indeed often

> "Listened to the song-bird's lay,
> Or watched him build his nest."

The ability to express himself in verse seems to have been almost inborn with Lowell. It is quite credible that he often wrote in rhyme because he had not time for prose. Indeed, he says it himself (in verse), beginning his "Letter from Boston":

> "Dear M. By way of saving time,
> I'll do this letter up in rhyme."

Even in these boyish days, his thoughts, such as they were, threw themselves into verse without effort. There is a capital letter to his friend Loring, in which he announces:

> "I'm readin' Burns the poet,
> And as I wished to let you know it,
> I thought the brawest gate to show it,
>   An' mak ye smile,
> Wad be (tho' far I fa' below it)
>   To try his style."

This rather elaborate movement is carried through nineteen stanzas, all scribbled the same day, despite a long interruption, through the arrival of a guest for dinner. This guest was the very young woman — perhaps his cousin — whose unrivalled charms the poem itself celebrates. The effusion is finished after ten o'clock that night, closing with an elaborate curse upon "Geordie," if he ever shows it! The end reveals no falling-off in vigor:

> "Or warse than a', may certain lasses
> Cut faithless Geordie as he passes,
> An' sternly eye wi' quizzin' glasses
>   The luckless swain,
> An' smilin' walk with stupid asses
>   To gie him pain!"

As to the young poet's accuracy in the use of mock-Scottish dialect, others must judge; but the versification seems already from a master's hand. His early fondness for Burns Lowell may have owed to his mother. She was of Scotch descent, while her mother came from the Orkney Islands. She taught Lowell to love the old ballads and legends, the myths and marvels of folk-lore. The poet felt that he inherited from her alone the romantic side of his nature. In the same boyish correspondence, Whittier is quoted and applauded for "sticking up for old New England." It is a pity we have not, also, one of Whittier's early attempts in Burns' dialect.

At this time, Longfellow had completed his five years as professor at Bowdoin, and, after a second period of European travel, had settled at Harvard. When Lowell, in 1838, was leaving college, a restless youth of nineteen, the elder poet at thirty-one was publishing his romance "Hyperion," and collecting his early poems under the dreamily fanciful title, "Voices of the Night." Whether he was ever actually Lowell's instructor, I do not know.

The young prince of Elmwood was a wilful student, striving to read everything *except* the books prescribed by his teachers, and cherishing a most robust dislike for mathematics. In this disposition to go his own way, and absorb whatever intellectual food he best enjoyed, he doubtless received encouragement from the Concord philosopher, who was the first to arouse his soul to loftiest ambitions.

The young Lowell, though chosen class poet, was absent at graduation. He was, in fact, suffering the penalties of rustication, pent up amid the "milder shades" of Concord. This doom befell him through his persistent neglect of prescribed books and tasks. There is a brief reminiscence of this stay in Concord in the "Biglow Papers":

"I know the village, though; was sent there once,
A-schoolin', 'cause to home I played the dunce."

His phrase hits the exact truth, as was his habit: due, perhaps, to the day of his nativity. Even the Faculty that reluctantly exiled him, knew how far he was from the *real* dunces. Emerson was kind to the restless boy-exile, and in their walks together showed him some of his favorite woodland haunts. The spiritual influences of the philosopher young Lowell as yet resisted. Indeed, this same class poem ridiculed the Transcendentalists, and also the Abolitionists.

But, before that very year ran out, Lowell not only secured his coveted "sheepskin" after all, but, what is far more important, had seen a great light, at least as to slavery. "A third party, or, rather, no party, is secretly rising up in this country, whose voice will soon be heard. The Abolitionists are the only ones with whom I sympathize of the present extant parties." So he writes to Loring in November, 1838.

By this time Lowell was already engaged in studying law. This was quite contrary to his own desire for a purely literary life. Mr. Norton, in his selection of letters, permits little light to fall upon this clash of wills. It was a time of much restlessness, as is made evident chiefly by later reminiscences. *E.g.* (Letters, Vol. I, p. 375, October 25, 1866), "I remember in '39 putting a cocked pistol to my forehead — and being afraid to pull the 'trigger," etc. The fearless frankness of this passage adds double force to Mr. Norton's assurance, given us in a happy phrase of the preface: "There was nothing in Mr. Lowell's life to be concealed or excused."

The impulse to poetry, however, asserted itself irresistibly. The first poem published, except some undergraduate effusions, was apparently "Threnodia," in the "Knickerbocker" for May, 1839. In the letters to Loring are always plenty of phrases like this: "I have many unfinished pieces in my head, which I must finish when I am in the mood." But we hear little enough about law, save a recurring resolve to abandon it. It is, perhaps, an illustration of a Puritanic conscientiousness, that he did after all finish his two years of legal studies, and took his degree in 1840. That he practised law there seems to be no evidence, save the title of a story, "My First Client," printed in the "Knickerbocker," in '42, and stigmatized as "pretty poor stuff" by its author seven years later.

More important events about the year '40 were his engagement to the gentle and gifted Maria White, — who greatly strengthened his ardor for abolition and reforms in general, — and the daring publication of a volume of poems. This book, called "A Year's Life," won for the young author little general popularity, but the full respect and interest of really competent critics. It practically determined his destiny, if this had indeed ever been in doubt. The title may be a reminiscence of Dante's "New Life." Love is the chief harper throughout. The prevailing tone, and the occasion of the title, may be heard in these verses of "A Song":

> "O moonlight deep and tender,
>   A year or more agone
> Your mist of golden splendor
>   Round my betrothal shone."

Less than half the seventy titles have been preserved, as "Earlier Poems," in the recent editions. Of these I like best "The Beggar." "Rosaline" is as morbid as Poe's "Annabel Lee," which it resembles. No one of these poems is really famous. Doubtless "My Love" is best known. There are in it echoes of Coleridge's "Genevieve," — especially one unmistakable line,

> "Great feelings hath she of her own,"

hardly an improvement upon

> "Few sorrows hath she of her own."

In general, these verses were for the most part, especially as to form, merely studies in poetry, after good masters, by a promising 'prentice hand.

About this time Mr. Lowell's father lost much of his property, and the poet was long dependent almost entirely upon his own earnings; but his poverty was a refined enjoyment of simple living, with the loftiest artistic and moral aims. His second volume of poems appeared in '43, and the rather stiff and pedantic, yet learned and witty, "Conversations on Some of the Old Poets," in '44. He was married in December of the latter year. This delicate and spiritual girl, Maria White, was herself a gifted writer, and was a constant inspiration to her poet. Their married life was a tender tragedy only nine years long. All lovers of Lowell know the verses, written after a little daughter's death, called "The First Snowfall":

> "Then with eyes that saw not, I kissed her,
>   And she, kissing back, could not know,
> That my kiss was given to her sister,
>   Folded close under deepening snow."

Lowell's study windows looked out toward the little grave upon the slope of Mount

Auburn, and over a picture in the study were hung in later days several pairs of worn baby shoes. For a second sister was soon laid beside the first. The poet's only son, also, is buried in Rome, where he died in his second year (1852). Mrs. Lowell sank under these fatal blows, and followed her children in October, 1853. These heavy griefs saddened but could not embitter the poet, who in old age could still say:

> "For me Fate gave, whate'er she else denied,
> A nature sloping to the southern side."

Meantime popularity and fame had come, with the appearance of the "Biglow Papers" in 1847 and 1848. The latter year marks the most wonderful productiveness and versatility of Lowell. Besides completing the Hosea Biglow series, he wrote the rollicking "Fable for Critics," with its keen, often prophetic, characterizations of all prominent American authors, including himself. He also, in a sort of poetic frenzy that lasted forty-eight hours, almost without food or sleep, composed the "Vision of Sir Launfal," perhaps the favorite among his poems.

But fame did not bring fortune, nor was Lowell destined to devote himself chiefly to creative literature. In 1857 he became Longfellow's successor in the Harvard chair of modern languages and literature, having first spent over two years abroad in hard study, chiefly on German, in which he had felt himself to be deficient. This chair he held for many years; indeed, I think he never has had a successor. In this same year, 1857, he became the first editor-in-chief of the new magazine, the "Atlantic Monthly." This chair he resigned to J. T. Fields in '62, but only to share with his friend, C. E. Norton, for some years, the control of the still more scholarly "North American Review." Many of his college lectures on literature were elaborated into critical essays, and, with others on political and personal themes, were afterward gathered up into the volumes called "My Study Windows" and "Among My Books."

Though patriotism, humanity, and love still inspired their minstrel from time to time, this critical, scholarly, and editorial activity was a heavy drag upon his poetic wings. Perhaps this is illustrated by the fact that his happy day at Chartres, in 1855, was not immortalized in the noble verses of "The Cathedral" until 1868. In the experiences of the war time, Lowell had taken an active share, in prose and verse. In 1865 he welcomed the returning heroes at Harvard, and sang Abraham Lincoln's praise in splendid verse. The tone of this "Commemoration Ode" was recalled in 1875–1876 by three other noble memorial poems. His diplomatic experience lasted from 1877 to 1884. His popularity in England among all classes was such as had never been enjoyed by any American before him. Perhaps the greatest accomplishment of his life was thus to draw nearer together the two greatest branches of the Anglo-Saxon race. But if any sane men had doubts as to Lowell's loyal Americanism, they must have been finally removed by the great Harvard oration of 1886.

There followed a few years of occasional poetic activity, but increasingly broken health, until his departure from the stage of life — it seemed, prematurely — in 1891. Holmes struck the note of general feeling in his verse,

"Thou shouldst have sung the swan-song of the choir," for Lowell was generally felt to be, — not only the youngest, but, — on the whole, the most loftily endowed in all the illustrious group of New England singers.

The Heart of the Singer

Lowell possessed in full measure the artistic nature. The furious rush of inspiration, with its wilful eddies and back-currents of indolence and procrastination, the impatience and tender affection at once lavished upon all the petty, confining details of life; the alternations of self-satisfaction and bitter doubt — all these he knew full well. They are revealed over and over, even in the discreet selections from his friendly correspondence only — not from his love letters — which Mr. Norton has published. But the rare flower of genius was planted in a vase — to borrow Goethe's phrase — of sturdy Puritanic manhood. His nerves were steadied and his blood purified for him by centuries of virtuous, peaceful ancestors. And the man never surrendered to the genius; nay, rather, the man's sense of duty encroached upon the higher rights of the dreamer! Whenever the note of repining is struck, in these frank, healthful letters, the regret is over the neglect of that supremest and rarest among all his rich gifts — poetic inspiration.

To a little circle of beloved friends, Lowell fully revealed himself: it was, indeed, a necessity for him. Toward the world he was suave, mannerly, but after all with a barrier of reserve that could not be passed. Doubtless a man like Longfellow, conscious that the inner gates are safely barred against all humanity, can more safely assume the manner of open hospitality to all. In these letters we can all see, at least far better than before, just how Lowell's work was accomplished. To be sure, the most precious part of the process remains no less a mystery; it is probably always a mystery, even to the artist himself. The noble "Commemoration Ode," like the "Vision of Sir Launfal," came to the poet almost as an instant inspiration, and took nearly final shape as fast as he could write it down; yet he had really been collecting the material and preparing himself to give it artistic shape throughout his whole life. It was only a process like crystallization that was at last so suddenly completed.

Until the memorable year 1847,—when Hosea Biglow leaped into sudden fame,—Lowell had won his way but slowly, like Hawthorne, toward the great heart of the people. This is not altogether strange. His poems are heavily, often too heavily, freighted with the results both of study and of thought. They are, to be sure, the sincere utterance of his soul, but they have not, as a rule, the simple, unmistakable melody of Longfellow or of Whittier. The taste for the best things in Lowell's earlier work, especially, is usually an acquired taste — acquired by loving study and long familiarity with him in mature life. Longfellow is oftener the companion of boyhood, Whittier the trumpet voice that startles our dreaming youth.

Love is a constant element in Lowell's earlier utterances, at least. Sound morality, perfect trust in God's wisdom and man's future, are chords never lacking. There is also, however, a vein of mysticism, which often darkens, though it does not perturb, the current of his thoughts. In this respect he is more literally than elsewhere Emerson's pupil. Thus, Emerson, gazing at Concord River, thinks at the same time of another stream: truth's current, or time, or human life, it may be (for it is by no means clear), and he sings:

> "Thy summer voice, Musketaquit,
>   Repeats the music of the rain;
> But sweeter rivers pulsing flit
>   Through thee, as thou through Concord Plain."
>   ("Two Rivers.")

This fancy is repeated by Lowell more elaborately in "Beaver Brook," and still again as he muses on his beloved Charles, in the "Indian Summer Reverie":

> "Flow on, dear river; not alone you flow
>   To outward sight, and through your marshes wind;
> Fed from the mystic springs of long ago,
>   Your twin flows silent through my world of mind."

To be sure, this perception of an analogy between an outward vision and a spiritual reality is not only the very essence of mysticism, but also, as Emerson, Longfellow, and Lowell all tell us, of poetry itself as well.

In the same way, Emerson's "Forerunners" expresses a feeling common to all poets,—perhaps to all men,—that our rarest and swiftest thoughts still elude our grasp:

> "No speed of mine avails
> To hunt upon their shining trails."

But Lowell could hardly have failed to remember his master's very words, when composing his "Envoi to the Muse":

> "I seem to fold thy luring shape,
> And vague air to my bosom clasp,
> Thou lithe, perpetual Escape."

Indeed, here, and in Whittier's "Vanishers," the similarity in words, and even in metre, appears to be a loyal confession of indebtedness; for within this generous-hearted band there are no mean jealousies or concealments.

Lowell's poetry always continued to be enriched by echoes and allusions from earlier singers. Often, indeed, this is frankly avowed, as when, beginning "Sir Launfal" with the words,

> "Not only around our infancy,
> Doth Heaven with all its splendors lie,"

he alludes plainly to Wordsworth's greatest ode on "Recollections of Immortality." But Lowell is in no sense a plagiarist, nor even vitally indebted, as Longfellow so constantly is, to other literatures. All he says comes warm from his own throbbing heart. He may borrow a word or phrase to utter himself, just because his scholar's memory has held and loved it, but he could have shaped his own expression at least as well. Often, in moments of deepest feeling, he strikes out a rugged, vigorous phrase, such as Longfellow's more silvery chime never strikes. This is especially well seen by comparing Longfellow's "Two Angels," written on the day Lowell's wife died,

> "And softly from that hushed and darkened room
> Two angels issued where but one went in,"

and the stricken poet's own "After the Burial":

> "It is pagan; but wait till you feel it,—
> That jar of our earth, that dull shock
> When the ploughshare of deeper passion
> Tears down to our primitive rock."

It may be said that here Lowell was the sufferer, and naturally spoke from the heart.

But that only points more sharply the difference in the two artists. Longfellow, after a similarly bitter bereavement, waited in silence *eighteen years*, and then wrote a tender and graceful sonnet, laying it away for his own eyes only! In fact, Longfellow uttered in tasteful verse almost every human emotion, *except* his own elemental feelings. There is but one slight love-note, for a living woman, in all his verse (cf. p. 135).

Among Lowell's close personal attachments, this intimacy with Longfellow is perhaps the most important. A century hence, this generous friendship may have become as prominent in the story of New England literature as is to-day, in our oldest home, the tie that bound together the poet-pair of Weimar.

Indeed, these two loyal friends, Longfellow the gentle, and impetuous Lowell, seem to me beyond question our two most important poets. Every mature American should have read all their works repeatedly. But while the tender sentiment, the broad human sympathy, even the sunny, genial scholarship of Longfellow might make a child think (most untruly) that he has mastered the full meaning, there is much in Lowell's verse which will utterly baffle us until our own deeper joys and sorrows furnish the key. Indeed, there will always be acute educated men (perhaps women, too) who will declare half his verses unintelligible to them. His own father was one such critic. Lowell is often essentially untranslatable, nor can his meaning be expressed at all in prose: a test Longfellow rarely resists so stubbornly.

As an artist in the technique of verse, in the combination of organ-like harmonies of sound, Lowell, when at his best, is unrivalled in America, and sometimes near to imperial Tennyson. Let him who thinks these words extravagant read, for instance, aloud, the twenty opening lines of "Sir Launfal":

> "Over his keys the musing organist,
>   Beginning doubtfully and far away,
> First lets his fingers wander as they list,
>   And builds a bridge from Dreamland for his lay."

A loftier music still is often heard in the "Harvard Ode," *e.g.:*

> "Our slender life runs rippling by, and glides
>   Into the silent hollow of the Past;
> What is there that abides
>   To make the next age better than the last?"

And precisely these two poems were essentially improvisations, struck off at a white heat, and almost at a sitting! Lowell does not always choose words so smooth gliding as those just quoted. The tones of the whirlwind, the surf, and the thunder are not those of the brook or the rain; but all are nature's voices. The severest test of this harmonic power is blank verse. Here Longfellow's "Divine Tragedy" often breaks down altogether into rugged prose, while "The Cathedral" need not fear comparison, at least in part, with the

> "God-gifted organ voice of England,
>   Milton, a name to resound for ages."

Indeed, there are not a few passages of "The Cathedral" which ring a clear and unmistakable challenge upon the Miltonic shield itself. We may choose almost at a venture:

> "His holy places may not be of stone,
>   Nor made with hands, yet fairer far than aught
> By artist feigned or pious ardor reared,

>   Fit altars for who guards inviolate
>   God's chosen seat, the sacred form of man."

One almost remembers these stately, slow-marching lines upon a page of "Paradise Lost"! It is interesting to note that Lowell, the most fastidious of critics, prone enough to self-dissatisfaction in all else, defends with unfailing confidence the metrical skill, the ear for harmonies, of Lowell the poet.

One quality, the one for which he is perhaps now the most famous, Lowell had hardly shown at all until the memorable year 1847. I mean, humor. That the Yankee has an abundance of the same dry, serious humor as the Scotchman, with much more self-consciousness and quiet enjoyment therein, is now very generally understood. (Though indeed Andrew Lang, Louis Stevenson, Barrie, and the other canny young Scots have nearly destroyed our belief in the incapacity of the Scotch to enjoy their own fun. The Yankee, at any rate, fully appreciates himself!) One of the closest and quietest studies of New England rural life, a half century ago, may be found in Hawthorne's American Notebooks, and it is remarked there that humor is a *universal* Yankee trait. The Hosea Biglow of the famous papers is in dialect, manners, etc., the typical Yankee; but of course his wit is such as no other Yankee, save the poet Lowell, could have furnished. The very first paper made a great hit, and presently all the country was buzzing with the refrain of

"John P.
   Robinson, he . . .
   Says they didn't know everything down in Judee."

The circumstances were happily prepared for such an explosion of enthusiasm. New England was bitterly opposed to the war with Mexico, which was really waged to secure wider territory for the spread of slavery. Whittier, like Lowell, had long been identified with the Abolitionists, but his poetry in their behalf had also been of the most earnest and strenuous character. There were ludicrous and extravagant figures among the Abolitionists, not to mention Abby Folsom, whom Emerson called "the flea of conventions." The laugh had always been against the reformers: now for the first time it was on their side. Of course, even now, the mirth excited was of a rather grim and sardonic sort. Mr. Robinson was himself an inoffensive man, unluckily caught out in the storm on the wrong side of this question. He is said to have fled to Europe, and finally to Malta, or even to Egypt, only to hear his own name chanted hilariously by strangers in the shadow of the Pyramids.

When the first of the "Biglow Papers" appeared, the remark of Charles Sumner was, that it was a pity the poem was not "written in the English language." Lowell himself afterward regretted the needlessly bad spelling, but held out stoutly for the antiquity and the poetic fitness of many "vulgarisms" and provincialisms charged against him. The ending "in'" — for "ing" — he defended especially as really more musical, though the professor and ambassador did not employ it in his own conversation! Many critics fully agree with Mr. Sumner's regret, at least as to a few of the poems. In the second series especially, written during the Civil War, several are dignified and even tragic, or rather elegiac, in tone. Here one can feel nothing fitting in the "lingo." Nearly all the peculiarities of pronunciation, though perhaps not all the rarer words, are still perfectly familiar in many parts of New England. The dialect adds a realistic flavor to the real drollery of the lighter pieces; but it seems quite out of place where the patriot poet is celebrating the heroism of his martyr nephew, the heroic General Charles Russell Lowell:

> "What's *words* to them whose faith and truth
> On War's red touchstone rang true metal,
> Who ventured life and love and youth
> For the great prize of death in battle?"

This quotation insists upon retranslating itself into "the English language," in which it was evidently composed! Lowell's friend and biographer, Francis H. Underwood, has evidently had the same feeling, when he quotes the strong lines written to remind England of the War of 1812:

> "I recollect how sailor's rights were won,
> Yard locked in yard, hot gunlip kissing gun.

* * * * * *

> Better that all our ships and all their crews
> Should sink to rot in ocean's dreamless ooze,
>   *   *   *   *   *   *
> Than seek such peace as only cowards crave;
> Give me the peace of dead men or of brave!"

The rustic dialect never coins phrases like "ocean's dreamless ooze!" But while we share Sumner's feeling, that some at least of these noble war lyrics should have been rescued from dialect, we regret still more deeply that we have not many another such bit of Yankee feeling and tenderness as "Suthin' in the Pastoral Line." We may defy any one to "translate" such verses as,

> "Once git a smell o' musk into a draw'" . . .

Lowell left unwritten, so to speak, a collection of tales in verse which he was intending to call "The Nooning." One only, "Fitz-Adams' Story," saw the light. That one has more of the local color, the wit, the homely feeling of old New England than can be gathered from all the graceful pages of the "Wayside Inn."

Lowell's best poetic utterance is generally

felt to mark our highest achievement in verse hitherto; but his poems are uneven, in the artistic sense often unfinished. Some of them, indeed, were prematurely printed before the vein of thought had worked itself out.

It is not incredible, then, that the call of patriotism has indeed deprived us of our rarest poet's unuttered master-song. If so, the more precious and memorable for us all should be the costly lesson of his life.

> "Weak-winged is song,
> Nor aims at that clear-ethered height
> Whither the brave deed climbs for light."

VII

HOLMES

THE LAST LEAF

THE recent departure of the Autocrat has brought freshly to the minds of us all the long peaceful career of this last survivor from the Round Table. It is a strange coincidence, at least, that from Bryant's birth to Holmes' death (1794-1894) was a hundred years to a month: a century which precisely includes the lives of our six most famous poets.

The gambrel-roofed house, close to Cambridge Common and the College yard, in which Dr. Holmes saw the light, most appropriately, on Commencement Day of 1809, was still standing until a dozen years ago. The new Gymnasium and Law School of the University displaced it at last. A few years later the Autocrat speaks of the well as alone remaining to mark the site. Perhaps that, too, has vanished. It is generally supposed the old house was pulled down about

1884. It is to be hoped the Autocrat died in that belief. As a matter of fact, however, the venerable abode of the race was cut into several sections, by a thrifty purchaser, hauled to the river side, and there doubtless it stands to-day, still unmistakable in its ignominy, tenanted by at least a half-dozen wretched families of various colors and races. *Books*, like men, "have a doom of their own," as Horace says, and Holmes has echoed it most effectively in his prelude:

> "O sexton of the alcoved tomb,
>   Where souls in leathern cerements lie,
>   Tell me each living poet's doom!
>   How long before his book shall die?"

But even he would hardly have had the heart to sing, in gaiety or earnest, the real fate of the house of the Holmes family!

The author's earliest memories of the spot are gathered up in the first number of "The Poet at the Breakfast Table," which should be read with Lowell's merrier "Cambridge Thirty Years Ago." Like Lowell and Emerson, Holmes was the son of a Congregationalist clergyman, a learned but not a witty man. It is said of the Autocrat, as of his younger townsman, that his poetic vein and his wit must have been inherited wholly from his mother.

At the dame's school of his childhood, Margaret Fuller and the second Richard H. Dana (who later spent "Two Years before the Mast") were among his mates. His last school year was passed at the Phillips Academy in Andover; and in 1867 a visit to these early haunts produced the sheaf of reminiscences called "Cinders from the Ashes." "The ghost of a boy was at my side as I wandered among the places he knew so well." But when at the station the elderly man called for two tickets to Boston, "the little ghost whispered, 'When you leave this place, you leave me behind you.'" Eleven years later, for the centennial of the famous Academy, these early memories were again recorded in verse:

> "I, whose fresh voice yon red-faced temple knew,
> What tune is left me, fit to sing to you?
> . . . Much could I tell you, that you know too well.
> Much I remember, but I will not tell." . . .

(Mr. Aldrich is not the only self-confessed Bad Boy in the Atlantic circle.) This clashing heroic couplet, by the way, the favorite of Dryden, Pope, and Goldsmith, was almost a part of Dr. Holmes' poetic second nature his whole life through. He began, indeed, to use it as a boy at Andover, in a metrical version from Virgil which is still preserved.

He entered Harvard at sixteen, and graduated without mishap, as all the world knows, in the class of 1829. Even in college he published some verses now famous, especially, "The Height of the Ridiculous":

> "I wrote some lines once on a time
> In wondrous merry mood,". . . .

and at graduation he was chosen Class Poet. This "merry mood" lasted, on the whole, through life, and in one of his most impressive farewells, — which were happily as numerous as Patti's, — I mean "The Iron Gate," read for a breakfast given on his seventieth birthday, he says:

> "I come not here your morning hour to sadden,
>   A limping pilgrim, leaning on my staff,
>   I, who have never deemed it sin to gladden
>   This vale of sorrows with a wholesome laugh."

In these college verses indeed we see little purpose further than to raise an idle laugh. But the man and the poet awoke suddenly in full earnest when, in 1830, it was proposed to break up the frigate "Constitution," popularly known as "Old Ironsides." Every American schoolboy shouted the lines:

"Ay, tear her tattered ensign down!"

written almost upon the instant by the youth of twenty-one, and published a day or two later in the "Boston Advertiser." They were copied everywhere, and were not only successful in their immediate purpose, but gave their author national fame at a single bound. These verses have still the place of honor at the opening of the standard editions of his poems. A recent article in "St. Nicholas" gives interesting information upon the present whereabouts and condition of "Old Ironsides."

We shall have more to say of Holmes' humor; but it is well to remember that this first great triumph was the clear, earnest cry of a patriotic heart. So the poet's own favorite, "The Chambered Nautilus," "The Voiceless," and many another masterpiece, even the Prelude "To My Readers," are wholly serious, almost sad. In the ability to bridge the narrow, but deep and dangerous, rift that parts humor from pathos, Holmes has, perhaps, no superior since Hood. He resents the suspicion that he is merely a jester more sharply than any other charge against himself. The singer is a true knight:

> "Think not I come in manhood's fiery noon,
> To steal his laurels from the stage buffoon.
> His sword of lath the harlequin may wield;
> Behold the star upon my lifted shield!"

For a year Holmes studied law, but this he abandoned more promptly than Lowell did later, and found his proper career in medicine. If we add the theological influences of his father's home, he thus combined an insight into all the three learned professions, which was happily utilized in the most successful of his three novels, "The Guardian Angel." After two years' study of medicine at home, he spent three years abroad, chiefly in the schools and hospitals of Paris. Doubtless this French experience intensified the clear-cut crispness and directness of Holmes' style, especially in verse. Of direct reminiscence there is not so much. "La Grisette," though Parisian in setting, has little of the Béranger flavor, save in its title. His welcome to Prince Napoleon, in 1861, with its "Vive la France!" has, perhaps, more warmth of feeling than most among his numerous songs of welcome and farewell. There are many recollections of these youthful years in the account of another pilgrimage, half a century later, "Our Hundred Days in Europe."

The year of his return, 1836, was an important one. He took his degree of M.D. at Harvard. He read his first long poem, "Poetry, a Metrical Essay," before the Phi Beta Kappa in August; and he published a volume of poems, among which this "Metrical Essay" was the chief. The very title, like the metre and the style, recalled Dryden and Pope. His rapid couplets here ring all the changes of feeling

> "From grave to gay, from lively to severe,"

though indeed Holmes never can be really severe, very long, save when attacking rigid

Calvinism in theology, or homœopathy in medicine; and even then the jest breaks through, just when his sternness begins to trouble us.

The connection of parts in this and in other sustained flights of Dr. Holmes' muse often baffles us. The clearness and completeness are always there — in the couplet or the stanza. His genius is distinctly lyrical. When he ventures beyond a hundred lines, on a single theme, his wings sag, or his course veers. As with his friend Emerson, the part is here sometimes more than the whole.

It might be supposed that poetry would have interfered with the young physician's success; but it was not so. Besides practising medicine in Boston, he wrote, during 1836–1837, medical essays which won three or four medals, offered as prizes in those years. Dr. Holmes has always had plenty of time!

After two years as Professor of Anatomy and Physiology at Dartmouth (the famous "small college" which Daniel Webster's plea had saved), Holmes returned to practise medicine in Boston, and to marry, in 1840. His position in the "best society" was never questioned.

His liking for the good things of life is confessed delightfully in "Contentment":

> "Little I ask; my wants are few;
>   I only wish a hut of stone
>   (*A very plain* brown stone will do),
>   . . . I care not much for gold or land;
>   Give me a mortgage here and there;
> Some good bank-stock, some note of hand,
>   Or trifling railroad share,—
> I only ask that Fortune send
> A *little* more than I shall spend."

He did not imperil his comfort by any premature devotion to abolition, or other unfashionable causes; indeed, there is a curious allusion to John Quincy Adams' gallant stand in his old age:

> "Chiefs of New England! by your sires' renown,
>   Dash the red torches of the rebel down!
>   Flood his black hearthstone till its flames expire,
>   Though your old Sachem fanned his council-fire!"

Here the "rebel" is the Abolitionist! Not that Holmes was ever lacking in frankness or courage. Fortunately for the reformers themselves, conservatism will always be in the majority; and Dr. Holmes was a natural conservative in many things besides his love of the heroic couplet.

In 1847 he accepted a professorship in the Harvard Medical School, and for thirty-five years gave there his four weekly lectures, resigning in 1882. His lectures were as clear and interesting in themselves as the subject would permit, and illustrated with such wealth of anecdote and ludicrous allusion as no other demonstrator of anatomy ever had at his command.

In 1851 appeared the first of his many poems for the class of '29. The next year he began a successful career as "lyceum" orator, with a course on English poets of the nineteenth century. This was in the golden days of the lyceum, and this course in particular had much of that consecutiveness which we claim as a cardinal virtue in University Extension. His favorite subjects appear to have been Scott, Byron, Keats, Shelley, Moore, and in a less degree, Wordsworth. He had a delightful habit of closing each lecture with a poem upon the poet he had discussed. Of these, the most loftily inspired is, without question, the elegy describing the drowning of Shelley, the finding of the body, with a volume of his friend Keats' poems thrust, opened, into his bosom; the burning of the corpse on the Italian shore, and the depositing of his ashes beside Keats' grave in the famous little Protestant cemetery at Rome. The closing plea against hasty denial of the divine grace for the anti-Christian poet is especially beautiful. Each quatrain of this poem demands a picture to illustrate it, though I do not know that it has ever been so published.

And now we once again approach the year which drew all these gifted New Englanders more closely about the Round Table of the Atlantic. Lowell, it will be remembered, was made editor-in-chief, with enthusiastic unanimity, when the new magazine was started in the autumn of 1857. His first condition was, that Holmes should be a leading contributor. The two were then already the most famous wits of American letters; but Lowell, though not yet forty, had ten years before leaped into popularity with Hosea Biglow, and also won supremacy among the critics by his slashing Fable for the guild; while Holmes at fifty, a prosperous physician and popular professor, was in literature little more than a welcome writer of occasional verse.

The late and sudden flowering of his prose genius is as wonderful as anything in his career. In three successive years of the magazine appeared the first two delightful volumes of "Table Talk," and the powerful novel, "Elsie Venner." After half a dozen years' rest came in rapid succession his happiest novel, "The Guardian Angel," and, in 1871, the third "Breakfast Table" book, "The Poet." The plan of these three volumes of table talk is so flexible, that everything is "in order," except, indeed, a motion to adjourn; for it is not easy to lay the book down, though it is really much better read piecemeal and thoughtfully. There is not much dramatic characterization in the conversation. We rarely hear any voices but Holmes' own; yet this one voice, in prose as in song, has "many keys"; sweeps, indeed, almost the whole gamut of human feeling and experience. Those of us not blessed with a keen sense of the ludicrous will miss much of the best in these books; but not all by any means. It is breakfast *à la carte*, and he is hard indeed to please who cannot find much both toothsome and strengthening.

In still another field of letters Dr. Holmes was to win laurels, though not the loftiest. His biography of Motley, the historian, appeared in 1879, that of Emerson in 1884. If anything was still lacking to prove his versatility, we might mention an impressive oration delivered to Bostonians in the dark days of 1863, insisting that the war must now go on to the end, even though that end should be the utter destruction of our people and civilization.

My last remembrance, as indeed numberless Harvard men's, of Holmes and Lowell, is as poet and orator at the great Anniversary in 1886. Dr. Holmes' hair was already snow white, as Lowell reminded him with tender playfulness, later in the day. But for years longer the little Autocrat was as familiar a street figure to Bostonians as the stately form of Phillips Brooks or the gaunt shape of Edward Everett Hale. His summers were spent in his pretty cottage on the favorite "North Shore," at Beverly. The inevitable end of the cheerful life tale need not be recalled.

It has been attempted to follow, thus far, a chronological outline of biography. A pleasant final task remains: to recall the charm of Dr. Holmes' literary work. The traits unmistakable in it are swift versatility, a crisp simplicity and grace, depth of earnest thought, but above all a merry, ever-present wit and humor. Holmes' medical writings, of course, lie outside our field; so, indeed, strictly speaking, do his two essays in biography, though that of Emerson is indispensable to our knowledge of both author and subject. It is amusing to see that Holmes, who was as little of a mystic as any true poet can be, seems to share in some degree the popular estimate of "Brahma," which many, at least, if not all faithful Emersonians place near the head of his verses: "To the average Western mind it is the nearest approach to a Torricellian vacuum that language can pump out of itself."

To the three famous volumes of table talk, a fourth, greatly inferior in power, "Over the Teacups," was added in his last years. The passage which will be remembered longest is the thrilling picture of the writer's sensations in advanced age: "At fifty, your vessel is staunch, and you are on deck with the rest in all weathers. At sixty, the vessel still floats, and you are in the cabin. At seventy, you with a few fellow-passengers are on a raft. At eighty, you are on a spar to which, possibly one, or two, or three friends of about your own age are still clinging." The yet more pathetic close of the paragraph need not be cited.

The opinion that Dr. Holmes' romances are chiefly breakfast-table chats still, is, I think, just, and, indeed, the general judgment of critics; but I am writing when fresh from a reperusal of them, and so am, happily, no critic. Their charm is so great and many-sided, that it is hard indeed to find any fault *while you read*. But there really are long stretches of monologue by the professor, while the story waits. The main plot is not skilfully woven, and does not show much originality. Indeed, in "The Guardian Angel," the heroine's fortune is restored to her by so hackneyed a device as the long-lost will, which the villain finds by accident, conceals while he strives to win her hand, and thinks he destroys before her eyes when rejected. Of course, it is only a copy. The real document is safe in the honest partner's hands — and all ends happily! Dr. Holmes himself knew how to ridicule this sort of thing, at least upon the boards, deliciously, as we may see in the Prologue:

" 'The world's a stage,' — as Shakspeare said one day;
The stage a world — was what he meant to say.
The outside world's a blunder, that is clear;
The real world that Nature meant is here.
Here every foundling finds its lost mamma;
Each rogue, repentant, melts his stern papa;
Misers relent, the spendthrift's debts are paid,
The cheats are taken in the traps they laid;
One after one the troubles all are past,
Till the fifth act comes right side up at last;
When the young couple, old folks, rogues, and all
Join hands, *so* happy, at the curtain's fall."

But in truth the chief value of these stories is to be sought elsewhere than in plot and construction. "Elsie Venner" is a rather grewsome account of a human being, changed in nature before her birth by the venom of a rattlesnake. Even this strange medical problem is of interest to the wise physician chiefly because behind it he sees a larger ethical question. As he says in a second preface: "Wherein lies the difference between her position at the bar of judgment, human or divine, and that of the unfortunate victim, who received a moral poison from a remote ancestor before he drew his first breath?" Not a promising beginning for an enjoyable romance, you say, — if you do not know your author. Yet it is as fascinating as anything of Rider Haggard's, and a thousand-fold more profitable to read. In passing, it may be said that one of the most delightful elements is the broad flavor of rustic Yankeeism, culminating in Major Sprowle's party. "Silas Peckham," the schoolmaster, is a merciless satire on the worst form of New England shrewdness and thrift. Students of the dialect will find here helpful additions to the vocabulary of Hosea Biglow.

"The Guardian Angel" treats the problem of heredity in a far more normal and pleasanter example. Myrtle Hazard, like every human being, is the complex result of many ancestral lives and natures. Through the eyes of the old doctor in the story, who in his ninety years has studied five generations of her race, we see a succession of her inherited traits rise to the surface and imperil her womanly life, until her own essentially healthy and noble nature comes safely to its own.

The last romance, "A Mortal Antipathy," is a far less serious and less powerful illustration of a kindred problem: the enduring force of impressions made upon the mind in early infancy.

We must pass to the poetry of Holmes. He is doubtless most widely known as pure humorist. "The September Gale," "The Deacon's One Hoss Shay," "How the Old Horse Won the Bet," "The Broomstick Train," usually come first to our minds. Nor is this altogether unreasonable on our part. Holmes' most unique gift to literature is his pure fun and wit. But it is actually a gift *to literature:* that is, it appears, often, at least, as an inseparable element in the composition of enduring masterpieces, which, of course, possess other and higher qualities. Even the "One Hoss Shay" itself could only have been written by a master of sentiment and pathos. Where else do we hear so effectively indicated the terrible gliding, slipping, passing of the years, the ceaseless flight of time?

> "Colts grew horses, beards turned gray,
> Deacon and deaconess dropped away,
> Children and grandchildren — where were they?
> But there stood the wonderful one hoss shay
> As fresh as on Lisbon-earthquake-day.
> . . . Little of all we value here
> Wakes on the morn of its hundredth year
> Without both feeling and looking queer."

Indeed, we may say of the entire poem, that full as it is of humor, and even of fun, yet there is method and art and deepest pathos in't no less.

There is much more pure fun in Holmes' poetic output than in Lowell's. "Hosea Biglow," especially, never allows us to forget his purpose, to drive home a moral lesson, or even to aid the political cause which he thought the cause of righteousness as well. Dr. Holmes himself truly describes his friend,

> "Whose play is all earnest, whose wit is the edge
> (With a beetle behind) of a sham-splitting wedge."

"The Courtin'," again, is pure pathos, in a homely setting, and leaves us, at best, very like his heroine,

> " Kind o' smily round the lips,
> And teary round the lashes."

Indeed, Lowell's really aimless fun, on the rare occasions when it appears, is the mirth of the scholar quite as often as of the Yankee. We may instance the piece written for a Harvard Commencement dinner, which is largely unintelligible save to college men, and even drops into Greek for a moment. The same remark is at least partly true of the delicious epitaph upon the brothers Snow, oystermen, in "Cambridge Thirty Years Since," culminating in an exquisitely ludicrous citation from Horace, " Jam satis nivis ! " (enough of snow !).

But Holmes' fun was a very large part of his nature, and quite able to stand alone, in prose or verse. Not to repeat names of poems already mentioned, "The Ballad of the Young Oysterman," "Evening, by a Tailor," and plenty more are quite safe from any moral application. Single lines and stanzas from many of his poems have been made proverbial by their very grotesqueness, *e.g.*:

> "And silence, *like a poultice*, comes
> To heal the wounds of sound."

Sometimes, in mock-dignified language, he alludes to a most familiar rhyme or bit of slang:

> "Like the filial John,
> Whom sleep surprised with half his drapery on."

Fond as he is of the dignified heroic couplet, he will make it sing of things that would have shocked — not alone manly Dryden or precise Pope, but — even poor rollicking Noll Goldsmith. For instance, when he has received a "Modest Request" for a speech, a song, *and* a toast, all on the same occasion, he is reminded of the thirsty sailor:

> "'Jack,' said my lady, 'is it grog you'll try,
> Or punch, or toddy, if perhaps you're dry?'
> 'Ah,' said the sailor, 'though I can't refuse,
> You know, my lady, 'taint for me to choose —
> I'll take the grog to finish off my lunch,
> And drink the toddy — while you mix the punch.'"

This element of drollery, I repeat, is essential to our appreciation of the real Holmes. No less essential, surely, is the pure pathos and lofty aspiration of his religious and imaginative verse:

"Build thee more stately mansions, O my soul,
    As the swift seasons roll!
    Leave thy low-vaulted past!
Let each new temple, nobler than the last,
Shut thee from heaven with a dome more vast,
    Till thou at length art free,
Leaving thine outgrown shell by life's unresting sea!"

In a few poems, such as "The Voiceless," we seem to hear the drip of the author's very life-blood in the verse:

"O hearts that break and give no sign,
    Save whitening lip and fading tresses,
  Till Death pours out his cordial wine,
    Slow-dropped from Misery's crushing presses!"

But the complete charm of the poet is felt where these two elements, seemingly so diverse, are most completely fused. Perhaps the most perfect example of what is meant will be found in the poem, almost too familiar to be quoted here, which was the special favorite of Abraham Lincoln. Indeed, it is said that the great emancipator once gained his case, as counsel for a persecuted old man, by quoting the famous fourth stanza:

> "The mossy marbles rest
> On the lips that he has pressed
> In their bloom."

Strangest of all it seems, that Dr. Holmes himself should have lingered for *sixty years* to realize in full at last the prophetic closing stanza:

> "And if I should live to be
> The last leaf upon the tree." . . .

VIII

RETROSPECT AND PROSPECT

LOWELL, in his late essay called "Progress of the World," says of man: "He is a social animal, that is, an animal liable in various ways to make his neighbor uncomfortable." Perhaps those who think the Yankee the coldest and most unsocial of mankind, — even those who love him least or love him not at all, — would still include him heartily within this definition of humanity!

Physically, intellectually, morally, the Puritan is aggressive. He has colonized the great Northwest, or at least claims to have guided and moulded the colonizing masses. He has taken the lead in recasting and liberalizing the religious, the political, and the literary ideals of the common fatherland during the century now closing. He has played, or is playing, a prominent part, in particular, in that twofold agitation for human freedom which is yet only half successful, — if even so much. The sectional enslavement of black men has become illegal. The universal improvement and uplifting of the laboring masses is hardly even yet faced squarely, as the Sphinx of our generation.

Garrison and Phillips, Sumner and Whittier, all so irreconcilable as opponents, and sharply critical even of each other, were all Yankees. In the untiring cry of the impracticable Mugwump, as in the shriek of the Abolitionist, the nasal twang of the Northeast is still predominant. And of those, born or unborn, who shall lead the way, through ridicule and persecution, to the serious struggle and the final victory which is assured, though not, of course, in any form we now dream, for a Christian Socialism, a truer Brotherhood of Man, — it is a safe forecast that New England birth, or ancestry, will be the rule rather than the exception. We shall still welcome the George Thompsons and Harriet Martineaus of every land to the front ranks of danger and strife. But already far away in the future we hear the Yankee emigrant's hymn set to a new meaning; and when the song shall be raised anew,

> "We cross the prairies, as of old
> Our fathers crost the sea,
> To make the West as they the East
> The homestead of the Free,"

though it may be woman rather than man that leads in the clearest treble, it will surely still be

> "Entunèd in hire nose ful semylie!"

The popular poets and historians of New England stock have all died or grown old too early to be identified largely with the new moral and social ferment which we see about us. (Our beloved and ever-youthful colonel, T. W. H., should of course be excepted.) Even in the chief struggles of the first and second thirds of our century, for Liberality in religious thought and Liberation of the African slaves, these literary men's names are not those which come first to the lips. Emerson in purely religious speculation was perhaps merely the greatest disciple of Channing, and Whittier is overshadowed as an Abolitionist by Garrison, possibly by Phillips and one or two others. Indeed, both Longfellow and Hawthorne, as well as Holmes, were conservative by instinct, and reluctant reformers at best. But, at least, such lives illustrate strikingly that the Puritan is above all a man of the firmest moral conscientiousness, and that even when he develops the fullest artistic sense of the beautiful he is none the less an ethical teacher. "Beauty is virtue, ugliness is sin," is their reversible creed, as voiced by the simplest and most serious of them all, Whittier, the Quaker.

The work of this group includes the greater part of the purely literary productions in America which can claim to have enriched appreciably the book of the world's life: the chief addenda being the "Sketchbook," the poetry of Bryant, perhaps of Poe, and the great romance "Uncle Tom's Cabin." Yet the general result of any thoughtful review, such as I have here attempted, must be helpful (as Mr. Barrett Wendell has remarked before me) rather to modesty than to pride.

In particular, it is clear that no great epic or drama has yet been created upon our soil. Indeed, in these larger fields of poetry we are scarcely represented at all. And while nearly all our best verse is thus limited by its lyrical form, so our one great author of romance is master rather of psychological insight than of constructive creation. Hawthorne hardly reveals for us a world teeming with a life of its own, as Scott, or George Eliot, or Dickens, did. A comparison of the "Scarlet Letter" with "Henry Esmond," or even with "Lorna Doone," may indicate more plainly the lack we feel. Hawthorne has bidden us gaze, far more deeply than quaintly gentle Blackmore or half-tender, half-cynical Thackeray, into the mysteries of the human soul. But has he, like them, made the idealized life of another century fill again with forms and color and motion? Or has any American romancer accomplished this? Indeed, in our own day, the masterly short story, delineating a single incident, character, or even mood, threatens to crowd the novel and romance out of existence altogether. Yet this at least must surely be

> "but the pause of the tide,
> Between the ebb and the flow."

It is most curious and baffling, indeed, that we have thus quite failed, as yet, to do in literature just what we above all men are accomplishing in material things. Doubtless, the gift of large creative energy will yet be granted to our literary artists, as it has been to our makers of constitutions and organizers of states, — to our business men, — even to our architects and engineers.

In those richer days, our literature will also be not less, but more distinctively, American, since the epic, the drama, the historical romance, must have an adequate environment, a local frame as it were, within which its living men or women speak and act. Even Homer sets his heroes between the fishy Hellespont and an Ida shaped in earthly rock, though capt with Zeus-sent clouds; nor can even Œdipus' heroic figure, or his words of eternal pathos, permit us to forget the nightingales and olives of a real Attica, of a beloved Colonus. And here the "Scarlet Letter," "Under the Willows," or even "Snowbound" and the "Last

Walk" are more than prophetic. Of local color American literature will have more, not less.

Meantime, it seems clear that this essentially lyrical product of New England is also still essentially English. Our Anglo-Saxon men of letters give utterance to feelings, convictions, visions, at times colored and moulded largely by the life in the new home, at times so remote from it as "Sir Launfal" or "King Robert of Sicily"; but in either case perfectly intelligible, at least, to those who have remained in the older island-abode of their race. Many a village blacksmith of Surrey and Devon, surely, — if not of New Zealand or Australia, — drops a tear over Longfellow's lines, feeling that every word was written for himself. And to pass at once to the other extreme of poesy's many-keyed gamut, the most striking occasion on which the "Commemoration Ode" has been cited, was when it turned the tide of a debate in the British House of Commons. (See "Lowell's Letters," Vol. II, p. 306.)

One exception might be effectively demanded: the "Biglow Papers" are almost wholly local.

And they stand, also, at the head of — with "Hudibras," almost alone in — their class. But certainly political satire, particularly in dialect, is very far from the highest class, even if it be granted an unquestioned place within the world literature at all.

Surely it is mere loyalty to our bravest critic himself, thus to face the truth. Nay, to him, perhaps with a prouder gratitude than to any other, we utter his own words:

> " By the embers of loss we count our gains,
> *You and yours with the best.*"

It is with especial regret, and reluctance too, that the student forces himself to see, even in the noble, many-sided character of Lowell and its utterances in his verse, rather an inspiring prophecy for our literature than the triumph of highest accomplishment. But this same keenest of witty critics and sanest of men has himself foreshadowed, both in prose and verse, the same judgment.

> " New occasions teach new duties. Time makes ancient good uncouth.
> They must upward still, and onward, who would keep abreast of truth."

Or if we may draw from the last survivor of the little group a hopeful utterance of a kindred thought, let us remember that great poetry is indeed, almost always, the final flower of a complete national existence:

> "Be patient! on the breathing page
> Still pants our hurried past;
> Pilgrim and soldier, saint and sage, —
> The poet comes the last!"

NOTE ON BIBLIOGRAPHY

THE books upon our classical literature are so accessible, and so well known, that no exhaustive list is required. The most complete view of American letters is afforded by Professor Richardson's history. Mr. Stedman discusses the poets only, with the closer sympathy of a fellow-craftsman. The Stedman-Hutchinson "Library of American Literature" is a rich storehouse of copious citations, from Winthrop and Captain John Smith to our own day.

Longfellow's diary has been made the basis of an excellent biography by his brother Samuel. Lowell's letters have been edited in two stately volumes by Professor Norton, who has added brief biographical outlines. This most valuable book (Harper Brothers) should be reprinted in much less expensive form, and owned by every patriotic student of our literature. The authorized lives of Whittier by Pickard and of Holmes by Morse are entirely adequate, include copious citations from the correspondence, and may be regarded as final. No similar book can be mentioned on Emerson. The volumes of Mr. Cabot, Edward W. Emerson, O. W. Holmes, are all helpful. J. J. Chapman has just presented effectively a "modern" view of our great idealist. Still more is the final book on Hawthorne yet to be written.

Meantime we have his own copious journals, the works of his son Julian, Mr. and Mrs. Lathrop, and others, and the æsthetic critique by Henry James.

Finally, all students should confess a heavy debt of gratitude to one of the most industrious, modest, generous, and useful of American bookmen, Horace E. Scudder. To him we owe, chiefly or wholly, the careful editorial work upon the standard "Riverside" editions of our most eminent authors. In the last years the rapid appearance of the poets in the single-volume Cambridge edition has increased our obligations. Every student should prefer this form to the more familiar "Household," or the diminutive "Diamond." Each book contains a brief biography, helpful notes, chronological list of poems, etc.

Most of the works here mentioned are published by Houghton, Mifflin & Co., whom we herewith thank for cordial permission to cite freely for the needs of this Manual.

A HISTORY
OF
EARLY ENGLISH LITERATURE.

Being the History of English Poetry from its Beginnings
to the Accession of King Ælfred.

BY THE

REV. STOPFORD A. BROOKE.

WITH MAPS.

Large 12mo. Gilt top. $2.50.

NOTICES.

"I had been eagerly awaiting it, and find it on examination distinctly the best treatise on its subject."
— PROF. CHARLES F. RICHARDSON, *Dartmouth College.*

"I know of no literary estimate of Anglo-Saxon poetry that in breadth of view and sympathetic appreciation can be compared with this."
— PROF. W. E. MEAD, *Wesleyan University.*

"In this work we have the view of a real lover of literature, and we have its utterance in a diction graceful enough to make the reading an intellectual pleasure in itself." — *The Christian Union.*

"No other book exists in English from which a reader unacquainted with Anglo-Saxon may gain so vivid a sense of the literary quality of our earliest poetry." — *The Dial.*

"A delightful exposition of the poetic spirit and achievement of the eighth century." — *Chicago Tribune.*

"In Mr. Stopford Brooke's monumental work he strives with rare skill and insight to present our earliest national poetry as a living literature, and not as a mere material for research." — *London Times.*

"It is a monument of scholarship and learning, while it furnishes an authentic history of English literature at a period when little before was known respecting it." — *Public Opinion.*

"It is a comprehensive critical account of Anglo-Saxon poetry from its beginnings to the accession of King Alfred. A thorough knowledge of the Anglo-Saxon language was needed by the man who undertook such a weighty enterprise, and this knowledge is possessed by Mr. Brooke in a degree probably unsurpassed by any living scholar." — *Evening Bulletin.*

THE MACMILLAN COMPANY,
66 FIFTH AVENUE, NEW YORK.

A HISTORY

OF

ELIZABETHAN LITERATURE.

BY

GEORGE SAINTSBURY.

Price, $1.00, net.

NOTICES.

"Mr. Saintsbury has produced a most useful, first-hand survey — comprehensive, compendious, and spirited — of that unique period of literary history when 'all the muses still were in their prime.' One knows not where else to look for so well-proportioned and well-ordered conspectus of the astonishingly varied and rich products of the turning English mind during the century that begins with Tortel's Miscellany and the birth of Bacon, and closes with the restoration." — *The Dial.*

"Regarding Mr. Saintsbury's work we know not where else to find so compact, yet comprehensive, so judicious, weighty, and well written a review and critique of Elizabethan literature. But the analysis generally is eminently distinguished by insight, delicacy, and sound judgment, and that applies quite as much to the estimates of prose writers as to those of the poets and dramatists. . . . A work which deserves to be be styled admirable." — *New York Tribune.*

"The work has been most judiciously done and in a literary style and perfection of which, alas, the present era has furnished too few examples."
— *Christian at Work.*

THE MACMILLAN COMPANY,
66 FIFTH AVENUE, NEW YORK.

A HISTORY

OF

EIGHTEENTH CENTURY LITERATURE.

(1660–1780.)

BY

EDMUND GOSSE, M.A.,

Clark Lecturer in English Literature at Trinity College, Cambridge.

Price, $1.00, net.

NOTICES.

"Mr. Gosse's book is one for the student because of its fulness, its trustworthiness, and its thorough soundness of criticisms; and one for the general reader because of its pleasantness and interest. It is a book, indeed, not easy to put down or to part with."
— OSWALD CRAWFURD, in *London Academy*.

"Mr. Gosse has in a sense preëmpted the eighteenth century. He is the most obvious person to write the history of its literature, and this attractive volume ought to be the final and standard work on his chosen theme."
— *The Literary World*.

"We have never had a more useful record of this period."
— *Boston Evening Traveler*.

"A brilliant addition to critical exposition. Written in a finished and elegant style, which gives enchantment even to the parts of the narrative of a biographical and statistical character, the work illumines obscure writings and literature and brings new interest to famous ones. One of its great excellences is the easy transition made from one style of writing to another. The plan is distinct and well preserved, but the continuity between parts is so close that unity and coherence mark the work in a material degree."
— *Boston Journal*.

THE MACMILLAN COMPANY,
66 FIFTH AVENUE, NEW YORK.

A HISTORY
OF
NINETEENTH CENTURY LITERATURE.

(1780-1895.)

BY

GEORGE SAINTSBURY,

Professor of Rhetoric and English Literature in the
University of Edinburgh.

Price, $1.50.

NOTICES.

"Mr. George Saintsbury is by all odds the most versatile, sound, and entertaining of English literary critics, and his book is deserving of the widest reading. In his genial, yet just way of judging he carries us from Cowper to the writers of to-day, touchin all with the nimbleness of his wit and the general unerring accuracy of his opinions. — *Boston Traveler*.

"In the clear definition it gives to leading writers, its systematic groupings, and its appreciation of main lines of development, it is wonderfully illuminating. The judgments passed upon noteworthy writers . . . afford in combination a body of criticism that the student of English literature . . . cannot hereafter venture to ignore." — *The Beacon*.

"There can be no possible doubt that Mr. Saintsbury's work is one of the best critical manuals of the period which it covers."
— *Philadelphia Evening Bulletin*.

"It is an admirable book." — *New York Mail and Express*.

"Thorough is the term to apply to Mr. Saintsbury's book; there is the stamp of deliberate, scholarly research on every page. . . . Done so well as to make it extremely difficult to find fault, is the best proof of the excellence of his work." — *Commercial Advertiser*.

THE MACMILLAN COMPANY,
66 FIFTH AVENUE, NEW YORK.

www.ingramcontent.com/pod-product-compliance
Lightning Source LLC
Chambersburg PA
CBHW032112230426
43672CB00009B/1710